I0419895

HOW TO GET
TO GET
YOUR HANDS
OUT THE
LION
MOUTH

HOW TO GET
YOUR HANDS
OUT THE
LION
MOUTH

HENRY ARMINGTON

authorHOUSE®

AuthorHouse™
1663 Liberty Drive
Bloomington, IN 47403
www.authorhouse.com
Phone: 1-800-839-8640

© 2013 by Henry Armington. All rights reserved.
Foreword by Bishop L. Lawrence Brandon

No part of this book may be reproduced, stored in a retrieval system, or transmitted by any means without the written permission of the author.

Unless otherwise indicated, Bible quotations in this volume are from The Holy Bible, King James and New International Version.

Testimonies have been grammatically corrected and edited slightly.

Published by AuthorHouse   06/21/2013

ISBN: 978-1-4817-6287-8 (sc)
ISBN: 978-1-4817-6286-1 (e)

Any people depicted in stock imagery provided by Thinkstock are models, and such images are being used for illustrative purposes only.
Certain stock imagery © Thinkstock.

This book is printed on acid-free paper.

Because of the dynamic nature of the Internet, any web addresses or links contained in this book may have changed since publication and may no longer be valid. The views expressed in this work are solely those of the author and do not necessarily reflect the views of the publisher, and the publisher hereby disclaims any responsibility for them.

CONTENTS

This book is respectfully dedicated
to the memories of
Rev. Dr. Timothy C. Turner, Sr.,
A faithful friend and partner in this ministry.
While our friendship was short,
the memory of it will last forever.

ACKNOWLEDGEMENTS

The author wishes to express his gratitude to all his spiritual, emotional and financial supporters for their constant love and devotion to Henry Armington Ministries. In particular, he wishes to thank Ms. Ada Edwards for her love and devotion to the support of kingdom building. She has ensured the process of attracting lost souls remain alive as our Executive Director. For this, he is humbly grateful.

It is his prayerful aim this book prove value in the realm of managing your finances from a spiritual perspective so you won't become a snare of the devil through the lost of your money. It is only logical you not handle your finances in the future as you have in the past, if living beneath the poverty line is your present state.

DEDICATIONS

To the congregation of Central Baptist Church in Denver, Colorado, Northern District Baptist Association, Western State Baptist Convention and National Baptist Convention, USA, Inc., for their love and steadfast devotion in their support of our Evangelical Ministry;

To the various denominational churches across the globe who've allowed me to practice in teaching and preaching ministry;

To all our Evangelical Partners who've continued to financially and prayerfully support our ministry for thirty-four years;

And finally but not least,

To all purchaser's and reader's because without you we could not have accomplished another milestone.

KEEP THE DREAM ALIVE!

PREFACE

The Christian family has grown and evolved in many ways. Today, we provide individuals with a much broader range of services across a longer stretch of life than ever before. We have greatly expanded our offerings in recent years by adding additional ministerial services, economic development services, helping hand planning and a wider range of evangelical and outreach solutions, including but not limited to, prison pen-pals, convalescent home studies and cyberspace technology products.

The bar has been raised and we have taken bold steps to ensure the people affiliated with our ministry are best educated and most qualified in our history. We've placed an increased emphasis on training and development. This allows me to boldly assert; the readers of our material are better than ever and we're offering you more in order to meet your unique needs during all stages of life. We remain committed to helping you build relationships, reduce crime, and pursue your lifetime goals and dreams today and for all the days ahead.

At a time when most friends and family members are turning their backs on those with limited assets and middle-range income, we are offering more deserving families our unique care on a face-to-face basis. Our passion is planning. Our focus is you and the way you handle your finances. Our primary objective is to prevent or cease people from being affected by this deadly epidemic called debt.

"If I have but one life to live then let me live it as a gospel preacher; forward deployed and conquering the world for our Master"

FOREWORD

Threats of recessions, unemployment rates rising and falling, long-time, viable companies filing bankruptcy, the recent housing debacle and news of sequesters. These hot topics have been on the cover of every major newspaper across this country. Even more alarming, many of our friends, family and church memberships have been directly or indirectly affected. It has become more apparent now more than ever, we must teach our congregations more than Jesus Christ, crucified, died, risen and is the soon coming King. Our people are dying for a lack of knowledge about how to live beyond Sunday morning sermons.

I often tell the Partners at Praise Temple we are made to be *producers* and not *consumers*; and I teach them how to fish so they have the option to own the pond they fish in if they so desire. This is a paradigm shift in the way we think about money and how we choose to save, invest or spend it.

Dr. Henry L. Armington, Sr.'s book *"How To Get Your Hands Out The Lion Mouth,"* is today's anecdote for biblical principles to understand Kingdom economics. This awesome read will help you connect the dots from a position of debt to living Heaven on Earth debt free! Are you tired of living paycheck to paycheck and robbing Peter to pay Paul? "How To Get Your Hands Out The Lion Mouth" will assist you in your journey to financial freedom.

Bishop L. Lawrence Brandon is the Senior Pastor/CEO of Praise Temple in Shreveport, Louisiana. He is the Apostle of the Praise Temple family of churches which include locations in Louisiana, Texas, Africa, Haiti and Jamaica.

CHAPTER ONE

THE DANGER OF EXPOSURE

In corporate America, it is stated that the best way to climb the ladder of success is to become exposed to those in higher power. It is often mentioned in conversation in regard to financial freedom; if you desire a prosperous, elaborate and luxurious lifestyle then you may want to become exposed to the right persons in our society. Exposure is good in its place, but it can also be quite dangerous and deadly.

Everyone desires spending less money. For some people, that means first overcoming a shopping addiction. About 5% of Americans suffer from compulsive shopping and even more struggle with lesser forms of overspending, with more people experiencing problems with self-control. Being surrounded by a culture that emphasizes materialism exacerbates the problem. Seemingly, everyone wants a slice of the American pie: a nice outfit, a nice car, a nice home.

People feel impatient or entitled to live the life of the rich and famous. Those with shaky self-esteem or self-worth are particularly vulnerable. Signs of shopping addiction include the inability to stop oneself from making purchases, conflicts with loved ones over expenditures and lying about shopping. While many people love shopping, people who do so compulsively do it despite negative consequences, such as going deeper into debt. They might get a lot of enjoyment from buying the item, but by the time they get home they're uninterested. It's not about the acquisition of the item itself, it's about the experience of acquiring it. They get a rush from it.

In some cases, compulsive shopping overlaps with compulsive hoarding, in which people accumulate so much stuff that it interferes with their lives and living spaces. Treatment from professionals often helps and it takes about six months to a year to make significant changes. We try to do that painful work in therapy, to find another way to discover love and feel love because the average person doesn't want their problems exposed.

It is imperative one surround theirself with individuals who can help them without being so judgmental. People don't like to disclose they feel out of control and embarrassed by the amount of debt they have. Cognitive behavioral therapy that encourages people to understand their actions and the longer-term consequences can help. For instance, instead of splurging on pricey presents, families and friends can talk ahead of time about exchanging skills or favors. It can also teach people cleverness such as using cash instead of credit cards or not going to stores when they feel depressed or stressed.

Most towns and cities have Shoppers Anonymous, Debtors Anonymous or Overspenders Anonymous programs that operate much like Alcoholics Anonymous. Nevertheless, for some people, it becomes a spiritual path. Compulsive shoppers need to replace old habits and friendships with new, healthier ones just as I did to exit a twenty-one year deficit in four months.

I recall a pastorate assignment in Shreveport, Louisiana at a Cedar Grove church, following the release of a spiritual all-points bulletin (APB). I was so excited about being this blessed preacher and leading such an awesome group of people, but I knew I could not render the services effectively with so much lingering debt. After all, I was at the tenure of a twenty year United States Naval Career and things with my finances were worst now than when I enlisted in the Armed Forces.

Suddenly and out of no where, in the middle of a worship service one sunny Sunday morning, a young man entered the facility informing an usher of his plan to demise the pastor, and thereafter, blow-up the church building with some nearby explosives. My friend, you can only imagine what was flowing through my mind and it certainly wasn't the debt I owed to various lenders. However, my main concern from that very moment was to guarantee my finances were in order just in case of an egress. I had to start ensuring my family wasn't left behind to tackle my accumulated debt alone. This was the day I learned first-hand that exposure is good in its place, but can also be both dangerous and deadly.

In a familiar biblical story, John the Baptist was in full force of exhorting the people and edifying God. The people had awaited the Messiah's arrival to their land. However, when we caught up with John, he was in the vicinity of the Jordan River. It is at this location he's witnessed by others baptizing souls, wearing unusual preaching garments and exploring a new and improved peculiar style religion.

Due to his distinct exposure, several people mystified him with Jesus. He emulated a broke preacher with minimal resources performing ministry. His clothes were fabricated of camel hair with a leather girdle around his waist. Unfortunately, he didn't dine in restaurants with urban savor, but rather ate jumbo grasshoppers dished in wild honey. The worship and praise services held at his designated locale were inspiring to such an infatuated audience as he preached the same message every week and no one ever complained about hearing the same sermonic pointers. A message echoing, "Make straight the way of the Lord."

The height of great men reached are not attained by sudden flight, but while their companions sleep, they are toiling upward in the night. John said, "No, I'm not him! As a matter of fact, if he showed up in the wilderness right now as I speak by this pool of baptizing waters, I'm mighty afraid I wouldn't be worthy to stoop down before him and unlatch his sandals."

There are three dangers of exposure and it doesn't matter how well you are at what you do or how many times you have successfully completed them. The first danger is exposure can be distractive. John is out at the River of Jordan baptizing some of the most sinful people of his day when he is suddenly distracted by priest and Levites from the nearby church at the discretion of the Sanhedrin Council.

The local officials and church leaders had heard about his assignment and mission along with his method of preaching, but were angered by his unwavering counseling style. These priest and Levites distracted John at a time when he's doing what God commissioned and charged him to do. They came right up to the bank of waters when he was about to plunge a devilish man in the name that's above every name and says to him, "Who are you?"

The second danger in exposure is it can be deceiving. This preaching machine in the wilderness thought for a moment the locals would leave him alone since he already revealed to them that he's not the one they think he is. He just knew they would allow him to complete his mission and purpose in life. So, John confronts King Herod concerning his relationship with his brother's wife, Herodias. He had finally crossed the ultimate line of sticking his nose in the wrong person's business.

John did the Christian thing the Christ-like way by going to the king in private, hoping he would accept the exposure as a real man. He said to him, "King, I don't know how your parents raised you'll, but according to scripture that's nasty. It's not right for you to sleep with your brother's wife and everyone knowledgeable of your wrongness, including her daughter." Nevertheless, instead of the king complimenting John or giving him a special love offering to support his ministry so he may receive a prophet's reward, he turned to his mistress to get her opinion on the matter.

These mean-hearted and cruel people incarcerated the preacher with a tentative date to martyr him by death, cutting off his head and placing it on a platter at a birthday party in honor of his mistress daughter. It is evident that people may deceive you when right and wrong is concerned. I wonder what was really going on inside their brain when the decisions were being made?

The third danger in exposure is it can be deadly. John was content being a signpost, pointing the way to Jesus, though it cost him his life. He was fueled by the burning passion of kingdom building. He wasn't a coward. He stood on what he believed, though knowing that firmness will often lead to deadliness from those you assume are on your side.

If a man can write a better book, he can also preach a better sermon, make a better mousetrap or build his house in the woods, but the world will soon find him in their time of trouble. Just as John exposed Jesus when he said, "Behold the Lamb of God, which takes away the sin of the world"; if you are not careful, your debt will expose you. Even God exposed the begotten when he wanted to get our attention.

As stated by the late Rev. Dr. Martin Luther King, Jr.:

"If you can't be a pine on top of the hill,
be a scrub down in the valley.
If you can't be a tree out in the forest,
be a bush in the yard.
If you can't be a highway in the city,
be a trail in the country.
Be the best . . . whatever you are!"

Let your light shine at all times because someone is down in the "Vale of Deficit" trying their hardest to get home.

CHAPTER TWO

IT WAS A SETUP

From childhood we are taught how to succeed in the world of ungrace. "You get what you pay for." "The early bird gets the worm." "No pain, no gain." I know these rules well because I live by them. I work for what I earn, I like to win and I insist on my rights. I want people to get what they deserve, but Jesus' parables about grace teach a radically different concept.

In Matthew 18, no one could accumulate a debt as huge as the servant did. This underscores the point that the debt is unforgivable. Nevertheless, the master let the servant off free of blame. The more I reflect on Jesus' parables proclaiming grace, the more tempted I am to apply the word atrocious to describe the mathematics of the gospel. I believe Jesus gave us these stories to challenge us to step completely outside our tit-for-tat world of ungrace and enter into God's realm of infinite grace.

Everyone have been setup in life or set someone up at least once, in some form or manner, regardless of age or experience. Several people spend numerous hours in reflection contemplating on if it was their fault. We live in a world filled with despair and hopelessness with the state of unemployment on the rise, weapons of mass destructions transported across the sea lanes, a confused government brewing in the nation's capital between republicans and democrats and sniper terrorist constantly roaming our country without our knowledge of their exact location.

Our hope must remain firm in the higher power of supernatural abilities while trusting and believing God is quite concerned of our present status. No matter how much we attend church services and render due benevolence with our hard earned monies; an enslaved, oppressed and poverty-stricken people cannot move forward until they understand the nature of their struggle. Change is only an asset when their eye's of understanding is broadened and attentive.

God has wise counsel available for you to examine when facing a financial famine. He literally informs you to "Trust in him to supply all of your needs." By faith, he will sustain you if you follow his lead. I survived a financial famine or two and God always made a way. He led me right on through it all, but I had to learn to walk by faith in the face of my dire plight.

By seeing things his way, my priorities were rearranged. He directed the use of the finances he entrusted to my care. As I needed more, I trusted him for the how, when and where. I did without things I thought I could not live without. I learned a more meaningful definition of true success. Success is having little and making of it what is best. However, it initially seemed as though it was the greatest setup of failure by God. I asked my neighbors, "How could this be when he is the God of everything?"

Sounds strange, but every once in a while I look around and ask myself, "What on earth am I doing here?" Odd question, especially because I'm the one who put myself there in the first place. I undoubtedly have a very good reason for being there—wherever "There" is. And every time I ask myself that question, I shake my head at the obvious rhetoric because the answer is always, at that particular time, "I don't know."

Perhaps I marvel at wherever it is that I am because "There" isn't exactly what I thought it would be, or perhaps it's because simply having the freedom to travel anywhere I want is a providential American right. I also marvel at the ease with which I can get "There." With each new adventure and with every new road and bridge, even the farthest reaches of the earth are seemingly all within reach. And once you physically and mentally commit to having a nomadic lifestyle—be it for business or pleasure—all you need is to see it through. As any good road warrior will tell you: "If you're in, you got to be all in."

And so it goes that I put myself all in every time I'm on the road, which is often these days. I'll take in the sites that are sources of pride for a particular city or region because that gives me a sense of its values and ethics. Then I'll purposefully get lost and rely on the locals to point me in the direction of what they think an outsider should experience. Like clockwork, after a few hours, I'm no longer an outsider to them nor are they strangers to me. There's an unspoken appreciation for one another when you're inherently interested to teach. Your effort and enthusiasm will be evident and, in time, your travel experience will be heightened.

Remember, of course, that no matter how much you travel and how much you know about a region or country or major city, small towns out there still have their own way of doing things. The people in those towns are all too happy to invite you in and make you part of the family. Take a happening I experienced in Mombassa, Kenya for instance. The townspeople there invited me to partake in an annual festival cook-off, which was about as foreign experience for me as a moonwalk. Yet it was one of the most memorable experiences I've ever had and it made me appreciate the people, many of whom have been attending this event since before I was born.

It's imperative to consider the underlying desires of your heart. It has a name: placefulness, a term coined by Dr. Rob Britton, who holds a doctorate in economic geography and is about as seasoned a world traveler as they come. Placefulness is as unique as celebrating Thanksgiving in Las Vegas, making your home inside a historical landmark, watching professional basketball in Brooklyn, walking through a garden of ice sculptures in Dallas or exploring the intricacies of a street in Chicago that you've traveled a dozen times, but may not have taken the time to really get to know. And then there's my hometown of Jefferson, Texas that takes you to the homemade syrup products of T.J. Blackburn.

Make this season of a setup by God the best adventure you could ever encounter in life. Travel somewhere you've never been, even if it's not too far from your own backyard. Engage the locals.

Partake in their customs and traditions. Eat their food. Meet their families. Go and get lost for a little while. Then come home safely, even if you are forced to make the best out of a bad situation.

Do you remember the historical story told of Moses? Moses grew up in the Pharoah's palace as an integrated Hebrew even though he worked, ate, slept and lived an Egyptian lifestyle. It's impossible to be a friend to the enemy and the people of God at the same time. If your heart fears your oppressor more than you fear God, you will never receive the victory. This degrading thought will stop you from worshipping God freely when the opportunity presents itself.

The person on top very seldom feels sorry for the person beneath. The oppressor will always make it hard for you to make a logical decision since he knows that in order for you to start serving him; you must agree to stop serving another. His mission is to keep you under the bondage of his law of poverty even though God wants you to experience freedom through your personal choices. There're two sets of laws he possess: one set for you and the other set for himself!

The oppressor will always try to promise securities that don't belong to him, in the first place. The Hebrews had no land of their own while in Egypt than where they lived, that actually belonged to the Egyptians. They were captive in a foreign land, powerless, confused and dismayed without any sense of direction. This level of perception was destined to keep them ignorant, illiterate and in the darkness of life.

Your oppressor knows that if you ever wake up and smell the coffee or discover what's really going on, you are going to leave him by way of the vehicle of what some calls "The midnight train to Georgia" as your escape machinery device. His aim is to keep you right where he has you for the rest of your days, but God is informing you that it's only a setup for a temporary stay to get you ready for greatness.

The Hebrews were rallied by a leader with vision, purposed mandated and commitment to God. They had to define who and whose they were prior to making up their mind to leave from bondage. Once aligned in ranks, they marched out the Nile Delta from the city of Goshen in large numbers. God had now given them a calm peace and inner joy, mixed with a load of hope for a bright future in the midst of their despair to make the best out of a bad situation.

Israel had just left the land of Egypt, loaded down with cattle and plenty of loot that the Egyptians freely gave them. After all the hardship, Pharaoh had finally allowed Israel to go and provide a sacrifice to the Lord in the wilderness. It had not been easy. Many terrible plagues had derived: the Nile River turned to bloody water, infestation of frogs, gnats, flies and grasshoppers, cattle disease, agonizing boils, a horrendous hailstorm and complete darkness. These staged events did not move the king, but when the Lord put all the firstborn children and beast to death in Egypt, he relented.

As they stood at the Red Sea with the waters before them, and Pharoah and his army with chariots coming toward them from the rear; Israel was pinned next to the sea with a large force of Egyptian cavalry approaching quickly. Israel was despaired. "Because there were no graves in Egypt, hast thou taken us away to die in the wilderness? Wherefore hast thou dealt thus with us, to carry us forth out of Egypt?" they asked Moses. It was one thing when Moses and Aaron confronted Pharaoh themselves, but now the entire nation was threatened with an army!

Moses was unmoved. He said to the Israelites, "Fear ye not, stand still, and see the salvation of the Lord, which he will work for you to-day: for the Egyptians whom ye have seen to-day, ye shall see them again no more for ever. The Lord shall fight for you, and ye shall hold your peace."

Moses' confidence was not in vain. He lifted up his staff, the Lord divided the waters of the Red Sea and the Israelites passed over with the waters as a wall on either side. Moses reached back and grabbed Joshua, Joshua grabbed Aaron, Aaron grabbed Hur, Hur grabbed the elders, the elders grabbed their families and they all marched over the sea on dry land.

Meanwhile, the Egyptian army attempted to pursue them, but their chariot wheels became stuck in the mud, effectively trapping them in the sea bed. The Lord then commanded Moses to again raise his staff and the sea returned to its normal state, drowning the Egyptians. As the bodies of the Egyptian soldiers came ashore, Israel feared the Lord and trusted in him and in Moses his servant.

Isn't that like the oppressor? He would rather die trying to prevent you from reaching your lifelong destiny than to just allow you to workout your soul salvation in peace. Even though a setup, "Thank God" for your exodus because of your faith: no darkness can darken you, no winter can wither you, no evil can enter you, no sin can sicken you, no sorrow can sadden you and no pain can punish you.

God gained a powerful victory and attained glory over all Egypt and his power was even known in Jericho. He did not do this through the hand of Israel, but by his own hand. There is much that we can gain from this great story of God's redemption of Israel. God delivered his people from a foe they had no ability to conquer with their own force and led them on toward the Promised Land. Likewise, God has delivered us from our sins, a rival we could not conquer by our own strength. What God did through Christ on the cross and in the resurrection was like what He did with Israel: he did it by his strength and power, and we can only "Hold our peace."

Israel still had to take the step of faith and pass through the sea bed, being baptized into Moses, as Paul would later describe it in his first letter to the Church at Corinth. God's victory still requires us to act in faith and live in obedience. Despite God's great deliverance, that generation of Israelites died in the wilderness on account of their unbelief. Let us not be deceived into thinking

God's victory costs us nothing; let us make good on God's victory and serve the Lord today!

Did you know that God wants to make a trade with you? He has a standing offer every minute of every day and it's amazing how few of us actually take him up on it. He wants you to give him all your cares, problems and failures. In return, he'll give you his peace and joy. On top of that, he promises to protect and take care of you.

God really does want to take care of us, but in order to let him, we've got to stop trying to take care of ourselves and worrying about every little thing we can't control. Many people would like for God to take care of them, but they insist on worrying or trying to figure out an answer on their own, instead of waiting for God's direction. They wallow around in puddles of their own worry, wondering why God doesn't give them peace. God will give us peace, but we must first give him our worries.

We give God our worries by trusting that he can and will take care of us. By trusting God, we're able to rest in him, knowing that he has the situation well under control. Worry, on the other hand, is the opposite of trust. Worry steals our peace, wears us out physically and can even make us sick. If we're worrying, we're not fully trusting God and we'll never be able to experience his peace.

What a great trade! We give God our worry and he gives us his peace. We give him all our cares and concerns, and he gives us his protection, stability and joy. That's the privilege of being cared for by him. Because he cares for us, he wants us to live in peace and not all tied up in knots of worry. He has ways of guiding us toward peace if we're alert enough to sense his direction. Imagine that you're driving down a road. Along the way there are signs that provide directions or give warnings. If you pay attention to the signs and follow their instructions, you will safely reach your destination.

In the same approach, on the road of life there are spiritual signs along the way. In order to stay under God's protection, you must obey these signs that tell you to trust him and not worry. Don't be afraid; have courage. If you'll pay attention to these signs, you'll find it's easy to stay on course. You'll experience the protection, peace and joy that only God can provide. However, if you fail to heed the signs, you may notice that the road seems a little bumpier than usual and you aren't as confident in your ability as you once were. You may become anxious about the unknown things waiting around the corner and even veer off the road.

Anxiety is like putting on a heavy coat on a hot summer day. It weighs you down. It's difficult to move and stifling to wear. According to Webster's Dictionary, anxiety is "A state of being uneasy, apprehensive or worried." Sometimes this uneasiness is really vague—something we just can't put our finger on at the moment. All we know is that we're uneasy.

You and I don't need to be anxious about tomorrow when we have all we can handle today. Even if we manage to solve all our problems today, we'll just have more to deal with tomorrow and more the next day. Why waste time worrying when it's not going to solve anything? Why be anxious about yesterday, which is gone or tomorrow, which hasn't arrived yet? Trade in your worries today for God's peace. Remember, everything is going to be alright. It was a setup, but look at you now.

CHAPTER THREE

I'VE FALLEN AND I CAN'T GET UP

What happens when I mess it up? We've been talking about becoming a fully devoted follower of Christ for years and years and doing it with excellence, but what happens when I miss it? I ought to know about missing it because I seem to do it a lot. One of the things that I have learned about God's gracious spirit is that he knows me so well; he knows I'm going to mess it up and miss it.

The Psalmist says, "Though he fall, he shall not be utterly cast down: for the Lord upholds him with his hand." That passage of scripture is so encouraging to me because it doesn't say if he falls, it says though he falls. For me that means, it's pretty much a done deal that we are not going to do this perfectly. In fact, it's a very realistic approach to life to say that we're not going to get it right all the time. Maybe even a majority of the time.

If there's ever anyone who knows what it's like to mess it up and fail to get it right it's Peter, one of Jesus disciples. He was rash and brash, and often outspoken and too quick to act. It was Peter who denied that he ever knew Jesus when he was under pressure in the garden, as Jesus was inside on trial for his life. When Peter recognized that he had failed, he went out and wept bitterly.

I would imagine he did like many of us when we've really messed up and become aware of it, he beat himself up. It is both interesting and very heartening that after the crucifixion and resurrection, Jesus deals with Peter in ways to redeem and restore him. Jesus is extremely aware of his failure and said to him, "Let's re-center on the things that are most important. Let's get back on track. Peter, here is what's central. Do you love me?"

Three times Jesus asked the question as if anchoring Peter on the very foundation of the needs of his faith walk. It was a way of gracefully and lovingly lifting Peter up when he had fallen. In our faith walk when we find ourselves coming up short, some of us are pretty good at getting discouraged. Some may even feel that we just can't do it and slide into apathy or are tempted simply to give up. That's where this grace-filled presence of Christ is so very important. Christ comes to us, as he came to Peter and seeks to lift us up.

Friend, know that you won't do this perfectly. None of us ever will. What is important is that we continue on knowing that, as we fail, Jesus will lift us up, set us again on the right path as we are willing and continue making the journey with us. The gravitational pull of individual friendships can have an enormous cumulative effect on the quality of our lives. With growing numbers of people living alone, either by choice or circumstance, friendships can occupy the emotional space that other people fill with spouses or significant others. Friends can link us to broader social networks and help enrich our lives. At the end of the day, a friend can be the emotional oasis that makes all the difference.

"Friends are what make us uniquely human," says James Fowler, professor of medical genetics and political science at the University of California in San Diego. "There is no other species that interacts so widely with other members of their species. So right away, you know that when you're studying these relationships with friends, what you're really doing is studying what makes us unique."

After a career studying different types of relationships and their impact on well-being and health, Harvard relationship expert Lisa Berkman has developed a broad view of the relationships people need in order to thrive. There is no optimal mix of friends and family, or of intimate and more casual friendships. "You can substitute these things," she says. "People who have a lot of friends may not need a lot of family ties." Religion and other group interests also can provide tremendous emotional support and

15

human contact that fulfills our need for human companionship and reinforcement.

Solid friendships provide needed validation that a person is valuable and of interest to other people. "Relationships help people feel that they're worthy, that they are capable, that they can set goals and accomplish them, and that they can control their life," says Toni Antonucci, a professor of psychology at the University of Michigan. Antonucci has developed a structure of friendship represented by three concentric circles that she describes as very close, close and not-so-close, but still meaningful personal ties. The rings can play different roles, with strong and emotional ties serving some functions and less-intimate friendships filling other needs.

A person's inner circle usually includes close family members and friends who are thought of as family. Rosemary Blieszner, a specialist in aging and adult development at Virginia Tech, notes how common it is to hear someone say, for example, "My brother and I are so close, we are best friends," or "My girlfriend and I are so close, we're just like sisters."

"Close friendships display strong support and affection," Blieszner says. A close friend fills an invaluable role as a confidant, someone who listens and pays attention to you, is willing to help you and has shared interests. There is give-and-take and often a balance that doesn't put too much weight on one party.

Women, it turns out, are often better friends to other women and also to men. Women also engage directly in shared activities and derive value by enjoying their friend's experiences. Men, by comparison, do not interact as much and tend to base enjoyment of sporting events and other shared activities on their own experiences. "Men confide in women and women confide in women," Blieszner explains, "So I think women are perceived as better listeners." She borrows an observation from Paul Wright, a retired psychologist at the University of North Dakota, to describe how friends of the same sex interact differently.

"Given the ability of friends to make you happier or sadder," Fowler says, "It might be tempting to cull your network of friends to eliminate those who have a negative influence on you." "You might say, well, I'll just get rid of all my friends who aren't perfect and that's absolutely the wrong advice," he says. According to his research, dropping a bad friend actually raises the risk that your happiness will decline.

"Every friend makes you healthier; every friend makes you happier," Fowler says. "We're not talking about your 500th friend on Facebook. We're talking about your dearest and closest friends, and these people are hard to find."

Antonucci has a different view. Human relationships have negative as well as positive consequences, and a friendship that has turned toxic is not worth keeping. "Nobody can drive you quite so crazy as someone who is near and important to you," she says. One of the things people have to do is to learn when to give up on a relationship and how to do it.

"The good news about friendships is that they get better with age," says Karen Fingerman, professor of human development and family science at the University of Texas. It almost doesn't matter what relationship you're talking about. They get better when you get older. Older people are generally more happy and forgiving and less judgmental than younger people. They also are less driven by emotions and hormones and do a better job of controlling their behaviors.

The number and diversity of friendships tend to naturally decline in later years, and can lead to isolation and adverse effects on health and happiness. Psychologist Laura Carstensen, who directs the Stanford Center on Longevity, says, "People should consider paying attention to the diversity and ages of people in their circle of friends. This can minimize the serious impact of having all your friends die off."

Developing and maintaining friendships requires continuous attention. "Give-and-take is important," Blieszner says. Other elements of solid friendships, she notes, include paying attention to what's going on in a friend's life, seeking out and participating in shared interests and activities, and being able to confide deeply to a friend.

"People should learn to value relationships," Antonucci concludes. They will make them happier. And with longer life expectancies, they really have to think about the kind of life they want to lead. I think we underestimate how important it is in our lives to have relationships. So I thank God for all my friends, especially when I've fallen and seemingly can't muster enough strength to pull myself up.

There are three things we must do when we recognize Satan has pinned us to the ground. It's imperative we stop feeling sorry about our condition. When we find ourselves coming up short, several people are experts in getting discouraged to the extent of convincing themselves that they can't go on any further. I want to suggest that throwing up your hands in the midst of obstacles will not make your situation any better or the condition disappear.

Numerous individuals have contributed to several mistakes in life. They have experienced many setbacks and failures, allowing people and things around them to be the cause of their regretful enslavement. Jesus said, "I come that you might have life and have it more abundantly." He informed us that the adversary is always present to steal, kill and destroy your efforts. Satan's objective is to entice you to fall, and thereafter, keep you downtrodden.

The devil wants to keep you broke, busted and disgusted, as well as, unemployed and in a state of homelessness. He enjoys the fact that you have fallen and can't get up on your own. The key to his madness is, as long as he knows you're down and out then you are no threat to him or his friends. He has studied you and understands that as long as you are without, you will refuse to give

God all his tithe and offering. He wants to keep you right where you are, but now is the time to get up and dust yourself off.

I am sure you are familiar with the cliché, "If you continue to do the same thing, you will continue to get the same results." The truth of the matter is, because things around us are constantly changing, if we continue doing the same things, we will not get the same results. Instead, our once fruitful results begin to decrease and could possibly disappear altogether.

Here is one illustration demonstrating why. What store can you go to today with a dollar and get the same amount as you did ten years ago? Five years ago? Two years ago? One year ago? Either one of at least three things have occurred: the price for products has increased, the amount or quantity of a particular product once received decreases, or the quality of the products diminishes, making it less valuable. Therefore, those who continue to carry a dollar to the store in order to make a purchase are getting less, in one form or another, year after year after year.

Here's another example. What if your employer paid you the same salary every year, while consumer prices continue to increase? Because your paycheck stays the same, your purchasing power will decrease which means you will not be able to afford as many things in the future as you did in the past. If this trend continues, you will soon be in financial distress.

The same principle demonstrated in the above examples is applicable to our faith. We cannot possess the same amount of faith from day to day, year after year and then expect to get where God wants to take us. When our faith is stagnant, we are not growing or maturing in our relationship with Jesus Christ. By virtue of who we are and who's we are; we must allow our faith to grow.

We must be willing to step out in faith, to get out of our comfort zone and start responding to God's directions even if he is leading us to do something different, something so outlandish we haven't a clue what the outcome will be. Of course, doing the same old thing is comfortable, but consider what happened when Abram, Moses, Joshua, Jacob, Rahab, Elisha, Esther, Ruth, Mary, Peter, Paul and so many others who trust God. As a result of their faith; something different, amazing, marvelous and supernatural happened in their lives.

We must be willing to let our faith lead us to where God wants to take us. Let's get out of our comfort zone and move into the new territory God has prepared and destined for us. The good news is, God says, "I want you to have a fresh start and a brand new beginning in life because now is the time!"

As long as you are living in this imperfect society and keeping your attention span on your past, you will never reach your full potential. Paul, the apostle, stated that as achiever's, you must be eager to begin, "Forgetting those things behind and pressing toward the mark of a higher calling which is in Christ Jesus." Never fool yourself into thinking the journey is so easy that you can accomplish it on your own.

God is far more interested in your future than he is your past. Some people think he is stuck on their past. They think all God has to do all day long is remind them of all the wrong things they've done in life. There are those with similarity to three newly, ordained transitional deacons who went fishing together and when they became bored they decided to reveal one of their innermost secrets to the group.

One man said, "I am a liar." Yes, I was a liar when you all met me and I'll be a liar when I'm dead and gone. The second man said, "I am a thief." He says, "Stealing is in my blood so if you catch any fish to carry to your homes, you better not place them in the cooler with mine."

The third man quietly sat in the boat as if he had changed his mind about revealing his innermost secret. He had heard the other two deacon secrets and now it was his turn to reveal his. So he says, "I'm not sure if I should tell you'll what my innermost secret is because you may not want to go fishing with me again or remain my friends after today." Finally, after much discussion and convincing of their agreement, he says, "My innermost and yet worst secret in life is that I'm a gossiper, and I can't wait to get to church Sunday morning and tell everybody every thing you'll said."

Maybe that's where you are today in life or maybe you've had some financial, relationship and/or self-esteem failures? You feel you have so many mistakes and innermost secrets and have failed God so many times that he just would not lift you up out of them all if you honestly came forth and revealed it. Yes . . . you are a failure by nature and need the assistance of Jesus Christ, but the reading of the remainder of this book may be the lifeline you've been searching for to pull you into his safety net. "If you confess with your mouth, believe in your heart that God has raised Jesus Christ from the dead," you can literally rise up out of your circumstance.

Whatever is causing your continuous failing or future demise, I plead and beg for you to just "Let it go," "Get over it," "Go on with your life" and "Move from where you are—to the position you need to be." Just as Jesus Christ was raised from the dead by his Father; if you lift your hands, focus your eyes and cry out to God, "Father, I stretch my hands to thee," in the comfort of your dwelling, he will start raise you from your dead state. This action must take place right away before initiating the next chapter in your life.

CHAPTER FOUR

STRUGGLING THROUGH A STORM

So many times we make situations worse than they really are due to our anxiety. We must be reminded by the Holy Spirit that fear is not of God. You must have the courage to step out on faith and do the seemingly impossible: start your own business, go into the ministry, apply for that promotion or anything you've been afraid to do and you know God has called you to do—"Just do it!"

Remember, "Greater is he that's within you than he that's in the world." You have nothing to worry about! God has already worked it out for you. It may not come the way you think it should come or when you think it should, but remember to just "Calm down, shut up and quit tripping." He's working it out for your good in his own timing. Do not ask the Lord to guide your footsteps if you are not willing to move your feet.

Everyone goes through seasons when the challenges of life feel overwhelming. During these times, it's easy to be tempted to talk about how bad things are. Maybe you are facing a situation right now that looks impossible. Don't get discouraged and give up! God wants to do something awesome in your life. Instead of talking to God about how big your problems are, brag to your problems about how big your God is. Be bold and start speaking favor to your state of affairs.

Every day say, "Father, thank you that your favor is turning this around. Lord, thank you that your favor is doing remarkable, astounding and overwhelming things in my life." When you release your faith like that, you'll see God show up and do amazing things that you've never seen happen before. Go ahead and declare favor over those situations and get ready to move forward in the victory and blessings God has prepared for you!

One of the most difficult times to discipline our minds, mouths, moods and attitudes is in the midst of the storm. This is the period between hearing God's promise initially and then actually inheriting it. I like to call this middle time the "Crossing over" stage.

Jesus told His disciples, "Let's cross to the other side of the Lake." Not long after that, the men encountered a raging storm of hurricane proportions. In the midst of all this, Jesus was asleep. Frantically, the disciples woke Jesus up. He then spoke peace to the wind and waves, and they subsided.

Jesus' words, "Let's cross over to the other side . . ." remind me of the times in our lives when God speaks to our spirit and tells us things like, "Let's do a new thing," "Promotion is coming" and "Blessings are on the way." But before we know it, we begin to encounter a raging storm of circumstances that threaten to destroy us.

All of us experience the storms of life in varying degrees, and we all have our faith tested and tried. Why does God allow it? Because, we all must learn how to behave in the midst of the storm. It is not by accident that you have volunteered your services to aide others. I assure you that there are those in your community who are desperately depending on you to make a difference for the masses. You will be the resource responsible for crossing them over to the other side of life challenges and circumstances.

There was a time when you couldn't walk through the door of an evangelical church without being approached by four or five well-meaning believers who wanted to make you feel at home. Not only did Christians welcome strangers to worship, but churches had well-oiled visitation programs assuring that newcomers would receive friendly follow-up visits in their homes. Where has the hospitality gone?

A lack of hospitality toward strangers has crept into churches, where many believers feel safer ignoring those they don't know. Hospitality is an unglamorous subject that doesn't get much attention from the pulpit. The command from the writer of Hebrews to "Show hospitality to strangers" contradicts a protective society's warning to children to not talk to strangers. Yet, the apostle Paul puts "Practicing hospitality" on par with being "Devoted to prayer" and "Serving the Lord."

For the most part, we don't know what to do with visitors! And so, hospitality must be modeled from the top down. The biblical concept of it should be preached from the pulpit, taught in Sunday school and modeled by spiritual leaders. If the leaders model an attitude of hospitality, they can infect the rest of their followers.

If the church fails to provide hospitality then the responsibility of initiating genuine fellowship falls on the newcomers. Newcomers may have to be the initiators if they expect to feel welcome in a new congregation. Churches must continue to remind members of the gospel message of hospitality. For inspiration; look to the final sentences of the Acts of the Apostles, where Paul "Welcomed all who came to him" as he proclaimed the kingdom and taught about Christ.

It is in times as these you'll notice a smile on the faces of those in desperate need of your assistance through the move you've made. You will notice a sense of ownership through the concept and attribute of servitude during this endeavor. It does not require tremendous faith to begin a thing or end a thing. The beginning and the end are both exciting times, but the middle is the main ingredient in which we are indebted to get off the ground.

God is making preparation through each of us who have volunteered our time, talent and treasures to take something that was initially half-dead or too alive to be dead and too dead to be alive, small and insignificant, and he is about to magnify and enlarge it into something he can use for century's to come. As you allow this prophetic word to infiltrate you, your struggle through the storm will diminish.

It is evident the road up ahead is not designed to be an easy climb as you thought prior to commencing your travels in life. You, perhaps, made a promise to God that if he saved you then you would serve him the rest of your days on this earth. Since you have discovered the wording was easier said than done, you really want to turn back. You have heard the call of the old way teasing you, as you struggle to keep your head above the water pressures of life. Maybe the plague is homosexuality, lesbianism, whoredom, coveting, stealing and robbing.

It's when you stop struggling, the alarm should go off in your head with convincing power that "Hey, something is wrong up in here!" The struggle is likened to having the desire to serve the Lord with all your heart and at the same time serve yourself the most. You want to give the Lord your all, but keep a little back for yourself just in case you are forced to work things out on your own. Before accepting Christ, you had only one nature to deal with and no desire to please God or others.

Nevertheless, always in the back of your mind was the WIIFM question of, "What's in it for me?" or "What can I get out of this deal?" But when you accepted Christ with the desire to live for God wholeheartedly, the struggle through the storm actually commenced for a cause. It's essential you understand that when you received your new nature, your old nature didn't move out—it just moved over!

The old nature is determined not to let that new nature have complete control over your life. It is territorial and can not stand seeing somebody else like God ruling over what it once ruled, nor seeing you possessing joy and peace of mind. I hate to be the bearer of bad news, but you now have two natures living inside of you. One nature is like the good "Dr. Jekyll" and the other is like the evil "Mr. Hyde."

The Christian life is a constant struggle to not allow the old nature to dominate the new nature. That's why you are struggling through the storm! If you noticed, every time you try or setout to do good, evil confronts you from every direction with three enemies causing a continuous struggle.

The first enemy is the moral universe. I have fought many battles against the old nature. I must be honest in saying I have won some and lost some. If you check the record book, none have perfect records, but as we excel in our Christian faith walk there should be more victories than defeats. The road to defeat is not paved with prayer cloths nor are they bandaged with blessed hankerchiefs, but are rather wade with the Word of God.

If you plan on being victorious in all your future endeavors and ambitions, you will be required to gain knowledge of the Word of God. You may sleep near, on or very close to your Bible, but unless you "Study to show yourself approved unto God" and adhere to his teaching then you will never defeat the hideous way of the storm maker.

The second enemy is the devil, himself. He is so deadly that we love blaming all our misfortunes on him and his family. I have you to know it's not possible for him to do everything we have blamed on him. Unlike God, he can not be every where at the same time. He has to go to and fro, up and down doing his dirty work, but he is powerful when we are spiritually powerless. So it's not fair for him to carry all the blame for our mess!

The third enemy is ourselves. People of all race, ethnicity and denomination love dining in the finest of cuisine restaurant establishments, but also eat jump food between meals. This statement is of the truth with reference to the old nature's spiritual being. He likes to snack on things like: filth and garbage, dirty jokes and movies, lust and riotous living, bickering and backbiting, to identify he's our enemy. One of his greatest past time snacks is a big, oversized bowl full of gossip. If you really want to get him excited and chuckling just say, "Child I heard" and watch how active he becomes.

However, if you can remove him from his food supplier and resource then you may weaken him of his madness. As long as he is weak, he will never be an effective tool against you and you'll regain the victory. It's not enough to weaken and starve the old nature if you are not planning to strengthen and feed the new nature. Your new nature demands caring and proper nourishment in order to live a productive life through the storm. The only way this will happen is by feasting daily on the Word of God because your new nature can't stomach garbage or digest foolishness.

No wonder the apostle Paul stated, "O wretched man that I am! Who shall deliver me from the body of this death? I thank God through Jesus Christ our Lord. So then with the mind I myself serve the law of God; but with the flesh the law of sin." Though you must deal with this old nature, you can still experience victory in Christ our Lord. In Jesus Christ there is: affection for the afflicted, comfort for the confused, direction for the deceived, help for the hurting, recognition for the rejected and vitality for the vulnerable.

CHAPTER FIVE

How Long Must This Go On

Sometime our days can be so full and busy we forget how fragile life really is. It's easy to allow little things to creep in and steal our peace and joy. Maybe something doesn't go our way or someone says something upsetting. Even traffic can cause us to lose focus, if we allow it. We have to remember that each day is a gift. If we choose to focus on what's wrong, we'll miss the beauty each day has to offer.

Don't let the precious moments of life pass you by. Don't wait for holidays and birthdays to show people that you care. Remember, each day is unique and cannot be replaced or exchanged. You have been given time that can be invested or wasted, and hours that can be used or misused. That's why the Psalmist prayed to God, "Teach us to number our days." He was saying, "Teach us to value every moment we've been given." Daily as you keep a proper perspective, you'll gain a heart of wisdom.

In this world there will always be something enticing you to worry. That is the nature of a fallen, fractured planet: things are not as they should be. So the temptation to be anxious is constantly with you, trying to worm its way into your mind. The best defense is continual communication with God, richly seasoned with thanksgiving. Awareness of his presence fills your mind with light and peace, leaving no room for fear. This awareness lifts you up above your circumstances, enabling you to see problems from his perspective. As you live closer to him, you will be able to keep the wolves of worry at bay.

A little boy wanted to meet God. He knew it was a long trip to where God lived, so he packed his suitcase with a bag of potato chips and a six-pack of root beer and started his journey. When he had gone about three blocks, he met an old man. He was sitting in the park, just staring at some pigeons. The boy sat down next to him and opened his suitcase. He was about to take a drink from his root beer when he noticed that the old man looked hungry, so he offered him some chips. He gratefully accepted it and smiled at him.

His smile was so pretty that the boy wanted to see it again, so he offered him a root beer. Again, he smiled at him. The boy was delighted! They sat there all afternoon eating and smiling, but they never said a word verbally.

As twilight approached, the boy realized how tired he was and got up to leave, but before he had gone more than a few steps, he turned around, ran back to the old man and gave him a hug. He gave him his biggest smile ever.

When the boy opened the door to his own home a short time later, his mother was surprised by the look of joy on his face. She asked him, "What did you do today that made you so happy?" He replied, "I had lunch with God." But before his mother could respond, he added, "You know what? He's got the most beautiful smile I've ever seen!"

Meanwhile, the old man, also radiant with joy, returned to his home. His son was stunned by the look of peace on his face and he asked, "Dad, what did you do today that made you so happy?" He replied, "I ate potato chips in the park with God." However, before his son responded, he added, "You know, he's much younger than I expected."

Too often we underestimate the power of a touch, a smile, a kind word, a listening ear, an honest compliment or the smallest act of caring, all of which have the potential to turn a life around. People come into our life for a reason, a season or a lifetime. Embrace all equally! Have lunch with God, bring your chips and your frown, and it may turn into smiles as you await the direction of where he's leading you on this journey.

I have the greatest respect for anyone with patience. It's so easy to transform out of your character, but it takes a real person to remain who they were purposed to be under pressure. God encourages us in numerous ways, as he redevelops and repositions us. There are times along the way you will be forced to wonder and ponder in your mind, "Lord, how long must this go on?"

In the recording of Habakkuk, it is one of the few books in the bible that starts off with a complaint. This book doesn't commence with God's unmerited favor or celebrating the sustenance and strength of his sovereign power. It starts by addressing a complaint with mankind, "O Lord, how long must I cry and you not hear me! Even cry out unto thee of violence and thou wilt not save!"

I don't know of one person in our society that hasn't expressed this sentiment of, "How long?" When everything seems to go wrong, chaotic and dysfunctional, it will leave you wondering in the hurried anxiety state of, "How long must this go on?" Life can really become burdensome while waiting and hoping your experience will soon come to a climax.

What could go wrong had gone wrong! The fig and olive trees had failed to produce in its harvest periodicity. There were no sheep or cattle reproduced. The people were stuck slap dead in the middle of strange conditions and unknowledgeable of how to get things back on track. They depended on their preceding plan of reproduction, even though all had failed.

What do you do when everything you are doing isn't working? You have been praying and paying. Seemingly, no one in heaven is listening to your struggles or paying you any attention. You have been knocking on heaven's door with knowledge that someone must be home because you're able to vaguely see the glare from the lighting shining through the windows lattice. What do you do? How long must you wait? How do you deal with this interlude?

When your prosperity turns into poverty, good times turn into hard times, aspiration turns into sensation and blessings turn into burdens; we must learn how to deal with our defeated dialogue. How you handled things in the past may not work this time in your present. You may be forced to change your way of thinking in order to alter your dialogue for your future's success. The communication statement, "We never did it this way before" may be just the change you need to aide you through these hard times.

Otherwise, you will experience more criticism than evangelism, more verbal crucifixion than spiritual benediction and more bitterness than sweetness. It's advantageous you learn to deal with your defeated dialogue if you desire going higher than the altitude level you've traveled. Don't worry about your ears popping and your nose bleeding! Everything is bound to level off as you come out of your season because "No weapon that is formed against you will prosper," "You are the head and not the tail," "You are the lender and not the borrower" and "Greater is he that is within you than he that is in the world."

The second thing you must do is devise the direction of your destiny. Once you are done complaining and looking out the window to see whose coming to help you in your time of need, sit down in a quiet place and commence writing a plan of action. Seminars and conferences across this country are dealing with the term "Vision." Instructors inform their students, "Where there is no vision, people will perish." But your vision will never come into fruition and your dreams will become your greatest nightmare, if you neglect drafting a plan of action. If God never gives you the what, how, when and where of the direction to your destiny, you are bound to fail.

The third importance is becoming dedicated to the divine doxology. If you're going to prosper during your waiting period, you must unconditionally and thoroughly praise the Lord in your situation. When he grants you opportunities to transit through fiery trials, it's he who keeps his hands on the thermostat and his eyes on the clock that "You not be tempted beyond what you can bear."

A prosperous people are a praising people! If you are going to reach your full potential and spiritual maturity of perfection, you must force yourself to praise the Lord. If excellence is to be your culture, excitement your classification and expectation your climate, you must praise the Lord in every situation he allows or the devil presents.

So what: the figs haven't blossom, the fruits aren't on the vine, the olives have failed, the fields are bare, the flocks are cut-off and the herd will not grow. You can still praise the Lord! Praise him anywhere like Hagar in the wilderness, Jairus in the streets and Hezekiah in the bed. You can still praise the Lord! Praise him anyhow: short like the publican, long like Job and quiet like Hannah. You can still praise the Lord! Praise him anytime: in the morning like David, at noon like Daniel and at midnight like Paul and Silas.

When praises go up, blessings will come down! When your money is funny, praise him. When your pressure is too high or low, praise him. In spite of your circumstances and problems, praise him. In the middle of waiting on your test results from the doctor's office, praise him. Nevertheless, if you don't want to praise him, please don't hinder or stop anyone that does because in a regeneration measure for one's self-enhancement you should consider;

> "Yesterday is already a dream
> And tomorrow is only a vision,
> But today well-lived makes every
> Yesterday a dream of happiness
> And every tomorrow a vision of hope."

CHAPTER SIX

The Consequence Of Insanity

One of the most painful realizations I had when I started getting my financial life in order was that I wasn't earning as much money from my job as it seemed. Before you can calculate how much a job pays, you have to figure out how much it costs. Sometimes a higher salary can actually leave you with less time and money. My salary at the time of this alertness was about $40,000 a year, so let's use that as a baseline.

Now, on the surface, that's really good money. If I worked 40 hours a week for 50 weeks a year, I would be earning $20 an hour, right? Well, that's not entirely true. First of all, we have taxes and more taxes including, but not limited to, federal income taxes, state income taxes and federal insurance contribution act (FICA) taxes. Federal taxes would eat about 11% of my paycheck, state taxes would eat about 4% or so and FICA would eat about 2%.

Second, I had to pay for my commute. This was about 10 miles each way and it was the primary reason I owned a vehicle. So, let's tack on top of that a monthly car payment of about $200, about $40 a month in gas, about $30 a month (prorated) in maintenance expenses and about $40 a month in insurance, just to keep that car on the road. I also had to wear a nicer wardrobe. I spent $200 a year to make sure I dressed appropriately for meetings, conferences, and the like—and that's a low-end estimation.

I also ate at least two meals eaten out a week, costing $10 each. There was travel about three times a year, when many of my expenses would be challenged, meaning each of those trips set me back about $100 out of pocket. Not only that, there were many times when I would put in extra, unbilled hours to meet a deadline. I easily averaged 50 hours a week at work. Plus, there was the time I spent traveling—about 50 hours spent going to places I didn't want to be per trip. And there was the time spent commuting—about 40 minutes per day. There were also work-related meals and other activities to attend, eating an additional four hours per month.

When you start running the math on this, the equation starts to change. After receiving my $40,000 salary, I'd pay out $6,400 in taxes each year. I'd pay out $3,720 in commuting cost. I'd pay out $200 in wardrobe costs. I'd pay out $1,000 in extra meals each year. I'd pay out $300 in extra travel expenses. Suddenly, my salary became $28,380.

Now, I'd work 40 hours a week, totaling 2,000 hours per year, right? On top of that, I'd add 10 hours of unbilled work a week (over 50 weeks). Three hours of commuting a week (over 50 weeks), 150 extra travel hours a year and 48 extra hours of activities a year. This would bring my total up to 2,848 hours or an average 57 hours a week spent devoted to my job. My job is suddenly paying me less than $10 an hour.

Of course, there were other job benefits that had some significant value, but frankly, I wasn't actually using them. My wife and I sat down and compared the health insurance offerings at our two jobs and my insurance was far better than hers, so we used my insurance. I had no use for her employer dental and beneficial life insurance option, either, and its retirement plan wasn't particularly strong. These things do have value when you're comparing jobs in this way, but only if you're using them.

Money can be a sore spot. Couples argue more about money than about sex, but not as much as they fight about the children or taking out the garbage. Nearly 84% of people note that money causes tension in their marriages and 13% say they fight about money several times a month. The leading cause of dissension is disagreement about financial priorities.

Husbands and wives divvy up money-related tasks along very traditional lines. Men still tend to do most of the big-picture, long-term planning while women manage the household's day-to-day finances. The gender divide seems to conform to some of our hardest-to-shake stereotypes of men hunt food and women make caves pretty.

In the poll's most eye-opening findings, men and women had dramatically different ideas about who does what with the family money and what their partners care about. Husbands were especially clueless, tending to underestimate how much women care about almost every financial issue, from saving for retirement to paying off debt. Several years in marriage and serving as head of the household and men still don't know what women want.

The gap between the financial issues that people care about most and what their spouse think they hold important may not be the Grand Canyon. But some couples will need an awfully big bridge to get across it. Women come much closer in gauging what matters to men. If anything, they tend to give guys too much credit, believing their husbands care more about paying off debt and saving for big purchases than men actually do.

As we sit and examine the greatness of God, we'll discover that due season has finally come to the Body of Christ through financial education adherence. Every group in the world has experienced success and accomplished their lifelong goals, dreams and ambitions, except members in most local churches. Several congregants possess spirits of anger and extended lives as debtors. The prophetic wording of the Psalmist, "This is the day the Lord has made and we will rejoice and be glad in it" is a psychological stability movement in the right direction as the Lord sends prosperity your way.

When tired of waiting and watching others receive their blessings, you'll do something positive concerning your present state to benefit your future. It's not coming to you, so you are forced to muster enough strength and courage to go to it! Most collection agencies operate as agents of creditors and debt consolidation. There is a logical reason for a 25% interest charge on a credit card.

Struggles and sufferings are to the debtor's advantage of the public requiring debt cancellation.

The definition of insanity is performing the same task, the same way and expecting new and improved results. If one thinks he or she can pay the minimum on a credit card debt and diminish its balance over night then that person is insane and only fooling oneself. The devil's methodical system is designed to vulgarize your progression efforts. Don't get it twisted! He will not assist you in accomplishing your financial goals.

Humans expend additional and unnecessary finances on various items including, but not limited to, clothing, jewelry, automobiles, houses and artifacts, but are too stingy to give God what rightfully belongs to him. There is a terrible virus that has penetrated the thought pattern of a vast amount of human beings. They desire stolen vehicles, merchandise and vacation luxury-trips for their personal entertainment. Their heart's are far away from giving God his belongings that they may continue retrieving blessings. This labels one as insane and in God's timing the person must suffer the consequences.

Ananias and Sapphira, a husband and wife, conspired to cheat God of his monetary substance on or after the sale of their land. There was a time people loved ministry to the extent of selling their personal property to improve and financially support kingdom building. They gave all their desired money to the church by laying it at the preacher's feet. These members of the church were taught and learned to adhere to the voice of God. When performing this action, they utilized the local preacher as a tool or instrument to retrieve their blessings from God.

It's imperative to analyze the race, denomination and ethnicity of the members at Ananias and Sapphira's home-church in comparison to those in our assembly. Research will aide in discovering the world's wrongness in terms of their giving. What church were these members affiliated? At their church no one never question the preacher's integrity, requested a meeting and financial statement or accused the preacher of misappropriation of funds. What kind of people made up this group of Christ believers and when are they coming back to the church?

The people were connected to the preaching and teaching of the apostles. As a corporate assembly, they honestly believed that since the preacher was at God's house, working for him as God's man, if error occurred according to the instructional source then God would deal with him accordingly. However, in every bushel you are bound to have at least two bad apples. This married couple assumed they could give God a percentage of the sale's funding and retain the excess for themselves, but everything living and breathing has its season.

Peter, the preacher, asked Ananias concerning the sale of the land, "Where is the extra-money you didn't turn in?" "Why have you allowed Satan to fill your heart to lie to the Holy Ghost?" "It was in your power to give all the funds from the transaction since you are the man of the house." "You want to be the BIG Kahuna, Ananias!" "Where is the rest of the money from the sale of the land?" God's word is truth and everything else is a lie. What's done in the dark will come to the light because everything will always be revealed sooner or later.

Prior to Ananias giving Peter an answer, he dropped dead at the place he was expected to lay the other fraction of currency—at the preacher's feet. Young strong and healthy men carried him out and buried him. Approximate three hours later, the preacher questioned his wife, Sapphira, being privy to the sale. She too lived long enough to give him an incorrect trade-sum of the property, preceding to her death and burial. This couple refused to give God what rightfully belonged to him as part of an initial agreement and at the right time, season and place, they suddenly died.

When you keep what belongs to God for yourself, it will cost you. You may think you are catching it right now, but just wait until tomorrow. God will place a curse on you that the devil himself can't remove. You have an opportunity every weekend to carry what belongs to him to his house, so hurry up before time runs out. If you fail, I assure you he has a way of retrieving his from you when you least expect. If you give him no other options, you will suffer the consequence of insanity because "The wages of sin is death."

When was the last time God saw you looking and evaluating yourself in the mirror? Everyone is pitiful, pathetic and their sins like filthy rags through the eyes of God. We are reluctant and timid in sharing our downfall and defeat with others. We don't want anyone to know that we are barely hanging on by the shredded threads of our faith with a "Thorn in our flesh."

Satan knows the location, angle and dimension of your thorn. His objective is to aggravate you by playing around with it or buffeting it with his finger nails. The thorn won't kill you, but eventually the infection will. If you don't deal with your "Thorn" in a timely manner, it may setup a viral-deadly infection with intense pain and over time grow more severe.

The thought of defeat can stir up feelings of anxiety, fear and depression. The longer you remain in your condition and refuse to direct your attention on the heavenly, the worst you'll become. God is coaching Satan as he twists your "Thorn" to enhance your movement. He has engineered a temporary defeat against you to get a more concise and clearer picture of your progress. Do you remember what occurred the last time you took a picture? The photographer gave the command "Say cheese for the camera" to get the real you from the photograph.

The Holy Spirit's aim is to lead us in the way we should go, but our actions don't always represent our true desires. Godly decisions require people with Godly courage. If you are going to endure life as a good soldier of the Lord then you may have to stand alone on the battlefield, but he will empower you with strength, wisdom and victory. When life sends you sprawling, your response is an excellent measuring stick for how mature you are in your relationship with Christ. You must have victory over defeat and weaken situations, as well as, a clearer understanding that God is ultimately in control of everything.

There's nothing more hope-filled than being given a second chance and a new beginning. God has plans for your life even when you mess up. He never stops loving you. When you are broken, shattered and smashed into little tiny pieces at the point of no return, he still never gives up on you. It is at that point he has your undivided attention, enabling you to see his purpose and plan for your life.

The world may be spinning out of control, crime rate may be climbing high up the scale and there may be wars and rumors of wars, but you can still have peace. If you give God your sorrow, he will give you his joy. If you give him your despair, he will give you his hope. If you give him your life, he will give you his principle and all your troubles will start diminishing. You'll have a new outlook on life along with an old traditional purpose-driven song to sing:

> "There's a bright side somewhere
> There's a bright side somewhere
> Don't you stop until you find it
> There's a bright side somewhere."

CHAPTER SEVEN

THERE IS PURPOSE IN YOUR PAIN

Have you ever awakened in the middle of the night because you had a great idea? So powerful is this idea that it is hard for you to get back to sleep because you cannot help but think about it. Perhaps you were driving alone in your car and a thought entered your mind that made you say, "Hummm!" Maybe you were sitting alone in your living room, relaxing and an inspiration came to you telling you to do something or take some sort of action.

These thoughts are your soul's way of communicating with you. Don't ignore it! God's trying to tell you something. I believe your thoughts are your angels sent here to watch over you. If you ever really listen to your thoughts, they don't usually lead you astray. That is if your mind is clear to start off with. I'm not talking about those individuals who claim a voice in their head told them to chop up their entire family. Those people have something else in them that we won't even get into here.

From this point on, listen to those thoughts. Write the thoughts down immediately. Don't delay. Get into the habit of carrying a notebook with you so when God starts trying to tell you something, you will be prepared to take notes. These ideas, inspirations and thoughts will help you discover your life's purpose. If you listen hard enough, you may receive a complete blueprint on how to live your life the way God intended you to live.

As workers for God, we have to learn to make room for him, giving him "Elbowroom." We calculate and estimate, and say that this and that will happen, and forget to make room for God to come in as he chooses. Would we be surprised if God came into our meeting in a way we had never looked for him to come? Do not look for God to come in any particular way, but look for him.

You should expect him to come, but do not expect him only in a certain way. However, much we may know about God, the great lesson to learn is that at any minute he may break in. We are apt to overlook this element of surprise, yet God never works in any other way.

If your life is continuous in contact with God, his surprising power may break out on the right hand and on the left. Always be in a state of expectancy and see that you leave room for him to come in as he likes. The disciples were sitting and waiting. Nobody knew who should take charge. Nobody knew who should lead.

This scene in so many ways reminds me of the United States of America when both President John F. Kennedy and the Rev. Dr. Martin Luther King, Jr., were assassinated during the same century. Everyone sit around pouting, "Our leader is dead," "Our leader is gone," "Whose going to care for us now," "Whose going to coordinate the marches," "Whose going to boycott against injustice," "Whose going to be our voice against racism," "Whose going to take care of those living in poverty" and "Whose going to do something about our present condition to get us to the place where we too can see the mountain top and hear freedom ring." If we leave room for God, there are so many things others have been doing for us that we can really do for ourselves.

We have more guaranteed days behind us than we have before us. There are some things and people we can live without, but we can't make it on our own without God. It's crucial we have him first and foremost in our lives to achieve genuine success. In everything we attempt to accomplish we ought to first, "Seek the kingdom of God and his righteousness" to acquire our proper quantity. It's possible to survive a few days without food and water, but you'll require God's salvation eventually.

The story is told concerning a captain serving in World War II. His airplane was shot down, crashed into the Pacific Ocean and he was forced to survive on his own for twenty days. But on the twenty-first day he was rescued. After being airlift from the cold swift waters and transported to safety by his fellow comrades, the captain volunteered in sharing to every veteran hospital his testimony of the crash, survival and rescue events. Sometimes we are dumped into an assortment of sea's to experience the fullest of life. If the captain never crashed his airplane, he may have been a longtime sharing any testimony of God's goodness.

Most problems have a history behind them. They don't just suddenly appear on the scene. Problems usually have a building up process. Things that should have been dealt with were left unnoticed and allowed to worsen or build up on it's own over time. As were through the grace of God and good works of the patriarch Joseph, according to the book of Genesis, the descendants of Jacob were allowed to settle in the country of Egypt. And even after the death of Joseph, the Egyptians continued to welcome them to their land.

Much of the leisure and liberty we enjoy today is because of the labor of the Joseph's who have blazed the trails for us. Many doors open are open because the Joseph's before us prayed, marched, protested and demonstrated. They were bitten by dogs, clubbed by law enforcement officers, hosed down by firemen and lynched by mobs. They opened shut doors and paved the path for us today. However, it is necessary now to blaze trails of our own. The Joseph Generation needs to live within each of us. If we don't keep the Joseph Generation alive, we will find history repeating itself.

It came to pass that the fame of Joseph was no longer remembered throughout the land. There arose a Pharaoh or king in Egypt that didn't recognize nor honor the accomplishments of Joseph. He had no regard for the prominent place Joseph held in Egyptian history. It didn't matter to him that once upon a time Joseph had been instrumental in keeping the nation from perishing. Neither did he have any compassion for the children of Joseph. He made the observation, "The children of Israel are more than us and mightier than we are. Come, let us deal wisely with them lest they multiply. For if we go to war they might take up arms alongside our enemy and fight against us."

The Hebrew's were in Egypt, trapped in the humiliating institution of slavery. Yet, Jehovah-God heard their cry and responded to their excruciating affliction. God specializes in getting stubborn, mean, adamant people to see things his way. He knows how to deal with the Pharaoh in spite of the Pharaoh. God wants to work through us, but because we are so stubborn, inflexible, intractable, unchangeable, stiff and unbending, he has to work in spite of us.

The real problem is one of unbelief. Circumstances don't overwhelm us because of their magnitude: they overwhelm us because of our unbelief. The real problem is not the size of our Pharaoh and his charioteers or the hugeness of the Red Sea. The real problem is when we simply just don't believe God. When we become overwhelmed by problems, the next thing we normally do is look for someone to point the finger of blame. It's typical of human nature to look outside to find fault than to lay the blame on ourselves. We hate to admit we are the ones at fault and wrong.

God has created each of us for a divine purpose. Some people struggle for years to find direction in their lives. If people could ask God one direct question, several would enquire about their purpose on earth. It is finding, knowing and living out your purpose that gives significant meaning to life. One of the most glaring waste of time and energy is living a purposeless life.

Once there were three trees on a hill in the woods. They were discussing their hopes and dreams when the first tree said, "Someday I hope to be a treasure chest. I could be filled with gold, silver and precious gems. I could be decorated with intricate carving and everyone would see the beauty."

Then the second tree said, "Someday I will be a mighty ship. I will take kings and queens across the waters and sail to the corners of the world. Everyone will feel safe in me because of the strength of my hull."

Finally, the third tree said, "I want to grow to be the tallest and straightest tree in the forest. People will see me on top of the hill and look up to my branches, and think of the heavens and God and how close to them I am reaching. I will be the greatest tree of all time and people will always remember me."

After a few years of praying that their dreams would come true, a group of woodsmen came upon the trees. When one came to the first tree he said, "This looks like a strong tree, I think I should be able to sell the wood to a carpenter" and he began cutting it down. The tree was happy because he knew that the carpenter would make him into a treasure chest.

At the second tree the woodsmen said, "This looks like a strong tree. I should be able to sell it to the shipyard." The second tree was happy because he knew he was on his way to becoming a mighty ship.

When the woodsmen came upon the third tree, the tree was frightened because he knew that if they cut him down his dream would not come true. One of the woodsmen said, "I don't need anything special from my tree, I'll take this one" and he cut it down.

When the first tree arrived at the carpenters, he was made into a feed box for animals. He was then placed in a barn and filled with hay. This was not at all what he had prayed for.

The second tree was cut and made into a small fishing boat. His dreams of being a mighty ship and carrying kings had come to an end.

The third tree was cut into large pieces and left alone in the dark.

The years went by and the trees forgot about their dreams. Then one day, a man and woman came to the barn. She gave birth and they placed the baby in the hay in the feed box that was made from the first tree. The man wished that he could have made a crib for the baby, but this manger would have to do. The tree could feel the importance of this event and knew that it had held the greatest treasure of all time.

Years later, a group of men got in the fishing boat made from the second tree. One of them was tired and went to sleep. While they were out on the water, a great storm arose and the tree didn't think it was strong enough to keep the men safe. The men woke the sleeping man, and he stood and said "Peace" and the storm stopped. At this time, the tree knew that it had carried the "King of Kings" in its boat.

Finally, someone came and got the third tree. It was carried through the streets as the people mocked the man who was carrying it. When they came to a stop, the man was nailed to the tree and raised in the air to die at the top of a hill. When Sunday came, the tree came to realize that it was strong enough to stand at the top of the hill and be close to God as was possible because Jesus had been crucified on it.

The moral of this story is that when things don't seem to be going your way, always know that God has a plan for you. If you place your trust in him, God will give you great gifts. Each of the trees got what they wanted, just not in the way they had imagined. We don't always know what God's plans are for us. We just know that "His ways are not our ways," but his ways are always best.

In order to be identified as people of purpose, we must pull over and get off the freeway of our fast pace, jet-set and hurried lives to focus on the important questions of life. Questions like: "Why am I here?", "Why was I created?", "What unit contributions can I make to society?" and "What is my lifelong purpose?" Many people struggle with questions of this sort daily.

A critical periodicity in Israel's record had occurred including, but not limited to, battle defeat, captives of the Babylonians, foreclosure homes and destroyed tempers. It was the darkest hours in their lofty history. Several people wondered if God really cared or had purpose for their lives. He used his prophet Jeremiah, as he does men and women today, to remind people in difficult and dismal times that he's still the reigning God of the universe.

God's purpose some time causes you to go through difficult circumstances. The interesting concept of his purpose is the journey one must transit. The people God loved were carried away as slaves, captive in a foreign land through painful and oppressed conditions. He say's to them, "I'm the one who caused it to happen" so don't blame the devil. How can I be in God's purpose and his will when he's allowing me to experience so much pain?

You should "Thank God" for pain! If it wasn't for pain you could burn or cut yourself by accident with a sharp object without knowing you're injured. We need to re-evaluate the importance of this frowned upon word. Pain is the body's way of sending a message to your brain to inform you something is wrong, and requiring direct attention and correction. When God allows us to go through painful circumstances, he's informing us that something requires immediate consideration in our lives.

The Psalmist said, "Yea thou I walk through the valley." If you continue walking, it's evident you'll exit on the other side of through. When facing difficult moments, you'll have to make the best out of a bad situation or start griping, complaining and bickering. The choice is yours, but sitting around surfing on your seat of do nothing and gazing at the condition of others won't help.

God told the people who were experiencing hard times in Jeremiah's day to, "Build houses, plant gardens, get married and have children." This phrase has interpretation of, "You are going to remain in this for a while so learn how to deal with it." You must become productive and patient in order to expect success when going through a fiery era. It may last seven days or seventy years, but hold on to your faith that has proven stability through the test of time. In spite of paying your tithes and a generous offering, praying and coming to church regularly or occasionally; can your substance of faith stand the heated test? Will you still shout and witness to your environment surroundings about God in accordance to your spiritual belief of "Thou he slay me, yet will I trust him?"

Just remember, how it end will be greater than how it started. You may have started on drugs, but ended in church. You may have started in the club, but ended in the choir. You may have started a pimp, but ended a preacher. You may have started a derelict, but ended a deacon. But whatever you were in the past, today, you are "More than a conqueror" and at times don't even realize it. God has a bright future awaiting you if you just continue trusting and serving him with all your heart. It's not over until God says it's over, so hold on because help is on the way as the dust settles.

CHAPTER EIGHT

AFTER THE DUST SETTLES

Several people spend their entire life in an attempt to accumulate resources in hope to soon become wealthy and famous. Many people have a misconception about their place in the income hierarchy. The Census Bureau has announced that median household income in the United States has fallen to $50,054 and the lowest since 1996 and down 1.5 percent from 2010. The announcement was the latest in a series of indicators that shows American households are making less than they have in the past. Median household income is defined as the dividing line for U.S. incomes—half of Americans make more than the median, while half make less.

The drop has an impact on politics. Political parties normally sell the idea that President's aren't doing enough to improve the economy. In elections focused on the economy, it's likely that median income along with other terms like "Middle class," "Low income" and "Wealthy" are used to convince Americans to vote a specific way. According to experts and a large body of research, many Americans aren't aware of which one of these categories they fall into. Many believe they are better or worse off than they actually are and have misconceptions about how other classes live.

These misconceptions can lead people to vote against their economic interests and often perpetuate policies that make it nearly impossible to climb the economic ladder. People form beliefs based upon the data they gather informally and do not have the benefit of looking at a random selection of the population. The real issue is whether it matters or not. This factor is based upon whether or not people feel they have the power to change their lives.

According to the Census Bureau, 46.2 million people—about 15 percent of the U.S. population—currently live below the poverty line or the income level needed to make a bare-essentials living in the United States. This figure depends on a number of factors, but currently calculated to be an annual income of $23,050 for a family of four.

The next level of income is the middle class, a broad category that captures the vast majority of Americans. It's also controversial: scholars and studies define sections of the middle class differently, but there are similarities between nearly all classifications.

The working class falls at the lowest end of the middle-class spectrum. These workers are employed in blue-collar industries or are paid by the hour. They typically have lower levels of education.

Next is the lower-middle class, which is primarily comprised of lower-level, white-collar workers. These workers typically have college educations, but lack the graduate degrees needed to advance to higher levels of employment. Income for these workers generally falls between $32,500 and $60,000.

Upper-middle-class workers typically have post-graduate degrees and work at high-level, white-collar positions. Household income for these workers is often above $100,000. According to the Census Bureau, upper-middle-class or professional class workers earn enough to be in the top one-third of American incomes.

The next income level is what is commonly called the "5 percent" or the percentage of Americans who make more than $150,000 annually. At the top of the economic ladder is the so-called "1 percent" or households that earn more than $250,000 annually. Few people are truly aware of their place in the economic hierarchy. Most people have only a vague idea of their income, based primarily on their income-tax returns, if they are filers. If they are not filers, they are in a large lower group that has only a vague idea of what their income is.

A person lifestyle can be deceptive in understanding economic class. A large majority of Americans live in the outer fringes of cities, suburbs and exurbs. Theirs is a life of low density and backyard barbecues. Many more people today compared to five years ago are having trouble paying the mortgage on this lifestyle, but it doesn't change their feeling that they are living a middle-class lifestyle. It takes a long time for people to change their view of what class they're in. That's especially true since the current definition of middle class is so broad that it excludes only the top 1 or 2 percent and the bottom 10 or 20 percent.

Popular culture also limits understanding of class, reinforcing the idea that all people are in the middle. Sixty years of universal television watching has fostered the idea that everyone is in the middle class. Most television sitcoms are about people like us, except sillier. There's very little media portrayal of a truly upper class that would make the vast middle feel that they were in some different sphere. Wealth has been a centerpiece for ages past and will remain a focal for centuries to come.

The upper and upper-middle class Americans describe themselves as happier, less stressed and healthier than lower-income Americans. They also made it through the recession relatively unscathed and report enjoying their careers more. Around 1 in 3 upper-class Americans say they "Frequently experience stress," while close to 6 in 10 lower-class Americans report doing so.

Stress is closely correlated with financial hardship: while just 7 percent of upper-class adults say they struggled to pay their rent or mortgage in the last year, 45 percent of lower-class adults say they had trouble making housing payments. Lower-class respondents also report being much more likely to lose their jobs, with a quarter experiencing a layoff or job loss within the past year, compared to 7 percent of upper-class adults and 12 percent of middle-class adults.

The better health of wealthier Americans also appears to reflect their access to healthcare: 45 percent of lower-class respondents say they had difficulty accessing or affording medical care within the past year, compared to 11 percent of upper-class Americans.

Not surprisingly, wealthier Americans also feel more optimistic about their future financial security. Four in 10 are very confident that their savings will last through retirement, while just 1 in 10 lower-class respondents said so. Meanwhile, most lower-class respondents say they are pessimistic about the future of the U.S. economy, while most upper-class respondents are optimistic.

Wealthier Americans are also more likely to feel like they're making progress in their careers. Those positive feelings apply to rich people personal lives, too. The vast majority of upper-class Americans say they are "Very satisfied with their family lives; just 57 percent of lower-class Americans say the same." Upper-class Americans are also more likely to be content with their housing situation. Still, wealthy Americans didn't escape from the recession without a scratch: Four in 10 said they have cut back on spending.

As for what poorer Americans think of their wealthier compatriots, many of their beliefs fall along the lines of expected stereotypes: respondents describe wealthy Americans as greedy and less honest than average Americans, but also more intelligent and harder working. Most respondents also say they think wealthy Americans fail to pay their fair share of taxes. Even upper and upper-middle class respondents say wealthy Americans pay too little in taxes.

Americans of all financial levels also agree that the gap between rich and poor has widened. The Census Bureau statistics confirm that observation. Still, respondents own self-identifications demonstrate the potential for economic mobility: just 1 in 3 self-described upper-class respondents said they grew up with similar privilege. A similar proportion said they grew up in a lower-class family.

While the amount of money it takes to feel rich varies widely by location, respondents estimate that a family of four would need to earn over $100,000 a year. Three in 10 thought they would need to earn at least $250,000. Respondents say it would take $70,000 a year for a family of four to be middle-class. That figure is far less than the median household income in the United States, which is close to $50,000.

A new year offers a fresh start! Whether you're ready to ramp up your earning power, start saving more money or manage what you have more effectively; this book is designed to help you improve every aspect of your financial life, from overall security to specific saving and spending strategies after the dust settles.

Planning exactly how you will reach a goal, such as saving more money, can actually make it easier to reach your financial goal. As you focus on your motivation behind your savings plan instead of the specifics of how it will be achieved, can increase the likelihood of success. Possessing a more abstract mindset can help people deal with unexpected challenges along the way.

For those struggling to make better money decisions, you may need to think about money as if it's a person. "How's your relationship with George?" as referred to President George Washington's face on the $1 bill. It may be of the essence to first examine your history with money. If you don't excavate what you believe and your sense of worth, you will be unable to progress. That history includes one's financial situation growing up and patterns of spending. The first step to fixing a dysfunctional relationship with money is to acknowledge its existence.

When someone asks for your Social Security number, question if it's necessary to share it. Never give it to a solicitor on the telephone or in an email, and if you ever notice a suspicious charge on your credit card, follow up with your card company. It could be the first sign of identity theft.

A lot of people have struggled over the past years, but the downswing doesn't have to be permanent. I turned my life around after running up in excess $20,000 credit card debt. I did it by ruthlessly cutting out "Extras" in my budget so I could focus on my bigger financial goals including getting out of total debt. Today, my past struggles are an asset. Since I'm a living proof, it is possible to make a complete comeback.

People who feel connected to their future identities are more likely to delay gratification. Take a moment or two to meditate on your future. Take deep breathes and release build-up pressure. Learning to live below your means will aide in diminishing your financial dust storm. Stop buying what you can't afford, even when you want to, and avoid debt at all cost or lower the cost of purchases to remain within your personal budget. For example, while some 25 million households own programmable thermostats, only half actually use them.

Many people don't realize they have valuable skills that others are willing to pay for. To get ideas for how to earn extra money, check out the services section on Craigslist and see what people are advertising—editing, gardening and event planning. Earning just a few hundred dollars a month can help get you back on your feet, plus you'll get valuable job experience and the possible start of a successful small business that you can continue to grow.

In today's economy, no job is 100-percent secure. Create a list of steps you would take if you were to lose your job, even though you hope never to have to use it. Having a "Plan B" can give you peace of mind, as well as, a practical "To-do" list if you ever face the shock of an unexpected job loss. Even in this economy, between 1.5 million and 2 million people quit their jobs each month. Storing up enough savings to pay for a year's worth of expenses can make that transition easier. Of course, toxic or depressing work environments don't always allow for that kind of flexibility.

If you're carrying around high-interest credit card debt, paying it off can save you a lot of money in the form of fees and interest. If you already have an emergency savings account and have the funds to pay off the high-interest rate debt, consider doing so. Some people avoid debt and credit cards to such a degree that they fail to build up a strong credit history, which can make it hard to get a loan when they want it, such as a mortgage. Recent college graduates with little credit history, for example, can get penalized when they apply for a mortgage or automobile loan. Lenders often want to see that you have experience taking on credit and paying your bills on time.

The easiest way to do this is by making steady, on-time payments every month and otherwise, keeping your accounts in good standing. If you pay your balance off each month, you should have a card that gives you rewards points. If you carry debt, just focus on getting the card with the lowest interest rate. Most people have multiple cards that aren't suited to their needs. Pick the one that fits you best and stop using the others. Don't close them, though, because that can hurt your credit score.

Socializing with friends doesn't have to be expensive. Surveys show that most Americans say they want to spend less and give more meaningful presents. When birthdays or other events come up, think about how you can give an experience, such as an afternoon at a museum or conversation over tea, instead of things. Most people fail to calculate exactly how much they're on track to save or how much they'll need.

It is essential to the health of your financial stability that you never over exert yourself money-wise having such a great time now, that you fail to consider your future. If you recall, when Joseph was brought before the Pharaoh to interpret his dream; he explained the meaning in such a way that the Pharaoh understood the interpretation, placed him over all his possessions and allowed him to ride in luxury. Joseph's interpretation to the Pharaoh is comparable to what I'm unveiling to you for your immediate action each month: pay your tithe (10% of your earnings), pay yourself in a designated separate long-term bank account (5% of all your income), pay all your bills (on time), splurge from the remaining funds and whatever balance is leftover the night prior to your last paycheck of the month—deposit these funds in the designated account holding your 5%. At the end of each day, you should save all your coin change for deposit twice a year (June 15th and December 15th) into your separate long-term banking account for accountability. Continuing these procedures consecutively for the next 10 years will give you bargaining resources for the duration of the next famine in the land.

Whenever you commence utilizing the talented-gifts God has granted you to make extra income, you will notice a radical change in your economic condition. If you take advantage of establishing a long-term financial goal, you will soon be an overcomer. Your situation may be chaotic, bills are increasing and collectors are ringing your telephone right now, but things will get much better after the financial dust storm settles.

The question may be asked, "How am I going to make ends meet?" "Who will help me this time?" The financial wind will cease once you organize and implement your own plan. I wish I could honestly tell you how long it's going to be before you get any better. I would prescribe three angelical salutations of "Hail Mary" and four glasses of cold prune juice, if I thought it would dissolve your obstacles. I thought about getting you to drink a coke since it's proven according to the beverage analysis to add life, swallow a BC Powder, and lie down and rest your nerves. Unfortunately, none of these will ease anything on a permanent basis, but if you just hold out and keep the faith through the night then in the morning everything is going to be alright.

There are times when we are moving too fast in the wrong direction and for the wrong cause. When things seem so dark and dreary with extended long nights, "Be still and know that God is still God" in the midst of your circumstances as he lightens your load while depressurizing you of unnecessary stress. Check yourself before you wreck yourself by your own actions.

CHAPTER NINE

I Can Holler If I Want To

It is fairly well known that, on average, women outlive men. What isn't as widely covered is that once the men pass, there is a significant economic gap, leaving surviving widows hanging on a financial precipice. A study of Census Bureau data shows that over 50 percent of women over the age of 65 do not have sufficient financial resources to survive the deaths of their spouses. There are some major causes for this financial insecurity.

Women suffered from wage inequality over the years, meaning that they both earned less over the course of their lives and also qualified for smaller pensions. When husbands die, the larger portion of Social Security income goes away and conversely, when the wives predecease their spouses, husbands suffer a lower loss of income. Since women live longer, they have a longer time to incur expenses and face a double whammy of lower income and higher total expenses.

There are economic benefits to marriage, such as sharing housing costs and, to an extent, transportation costs. However, rents, mortgages, and car and maintenance payments are often constants. Unfortunately, while identifying the problem, the aforementioned study doesn't actually make any suggestions for how to fix the problem. Certainly, the closing of the gender wage inequality gap will help, but that gap is not closed now.

Too often, individuals model out the expected bump in income provided by Social Security, but fail to account for the subsequent drop after one spouse passes. While research shows there is a 20 percent increase in the risk of dying within a year for the surviving spouse, the vast majority of surviving spouses do just that—survive. They need to prepare for the high likelihood that one will outlive the other and will have to deal with a decline in income not matched by a similar decline in expenses. Several are living in degrading conditions trying their best to make ends meet without enough public assistance.

There's a bible story of a demonic possessed man living in the vicinity of a cemetery near a town of people who were afraid to challenge his condition. Instead of challenging this gentleman to do or become better, the community avoided all communication and interactions with him. They were adjusted to his consigned unending irrelevance. But when they discovered him in the company of Jesus it confused them because the man had suddenly transcended from disgrace to dignity.

Some people are eternal spectators who only go out to see what others are accomplishing. They are normally found standing along the sideline of someone else's prosperity. America is a great nation, but our history records that as long as we were barefoot and laughing when no one was tickled, our enemies were satisfied. But one day, America looked up and saw our representatives standing before the Supreme Court interpreting the Constitution better than those who wrote it, marching to the voting booths, sitting at lunch counters and all of a sudden became afraid.

If you desire acquiring relief from your condition, you must do something about your present state as help arrives and presents itself. The world often views external scars and feel heat from burdens, but disregard perspective talents. When one is lost internally, they live on the edge of the danger zone of life without any true identity of who they are, how they got here and where they're intending to go. Their troubles rush through their minds daily without a shout or scream of release of those things enclosed called demons.

There are several people living in this United States, home of the free and land of the brave, but are still strangers in a bizarre land, as well as, poor pilgrims of sorrow. The historical moments and wings of their assigned angel will eventually touch their soul and awaken their curiosity. Once realizing God's presence above them, Jesus praying for them, angels all around them, and good and mercy behind them; they will commence singing the song, "I got a new name over in Zion and it's mine" with grand enthusiasm to leap and holler with assurance that brighter days are ahead.

When deliverance is relevant you need a radical change. A radical change denotes the end of something, the fulfillment of another and the beginning of a new day. Nevertheless, ones behavior will determine the amount of change in their state of affairs. Numerous years have past and changes have been attempted, but we still live in a crazy generation. A world that will send a child to jail—charged with juvenile delinquency for stealing a loaf of bread because he's hungry—and then give a man an award for stealing a bank, must be a crazy world.

Situations may cause you to holler when requiring help. Don't become discouraged or stop asking for assistance when in dire need! Everyone has required some form of aide at one time or another, but there's nothing any sadder than being dejected by your own family and friendship circle in a time of crisis. You need someone to vindicate you when requiring a breakthrough and a little peace in your valley.

When a person stands erect in the world, only the bottom of their feet touches the ground. The rest of them will be mingled with the stars, communing with eternity. I can adequately assume what happens to the individual's soul by borrowing an old saying from my grandparents: "I was on a downward road, no hat on my head, no shoes on my feet, no God on my side and no heaven in my view. I was too mean to live and not fit to die. The handcuffs of hell on my hands, the shackles of damnation on my feet, but the Lord spoke peace to my dying soul. He turned me around, cut loose my stammering tongue and sent me on my way. Since that day, I've been sometimes rising and sometimes falling, but I made a vow to the Lord that I'll never turn back no more. I'm going to run on and see what the end's gonna be." Holler!

CHAPTER TEN

The End Of Living Paycheck To Paycheck

You've probably heard it said, "It's not whether you win or lose, it's how you play the game." Do you believe that? I don't! Man was created to be a winner. The bible tells us so! We read in Genesis, for example, that man was originally put on this earth as a dominating lord. God gave him dominion over the earth and everything that crept, flew, crawled and breathed there.

In fact, man didn't even know what losing was until he separated himself from God through his own disobedience in the Garden of Eden. When that happened, the man ran headlong into defeat. He was forced to accept failure as his lot in life, lowering himself to a subordinate position—a position he was never meant to occupy. Now, you may be thinking, "I don't feel like a winner! I feel like a loser and I've got plenty of failures in my life to prove it!" If that's the case, don't worry. You just need a new attitude.

The epidemic of debt has impacted nearly every family in this country. According to some commentators and economic analyst, nearly 62% of Americans have no regular savings and most of them are in a $136,000 debt, without a clue of how to exit. It is evident that 70% of the people in this land are living paycheck to paycheck. It's obvious we've been on a spending spree, which signals we are materialistic to the core. My objective is to give instruction and guidance to people of all race, ethnic and income groups who are trying so desperately hard to keep a roof over their head, food on the table, utilities on in their home, fuel in the vehicle and manage leftover funds appropriately as an extra cash flow.

The relationship between money and happiness is one of the most interesting, but yet complicated task in the study of our land. Money can compel attention, devotion and lust for more. It can motivate minds, capture wills and divide hearts. It is considered to many as a rival god as revealed in the statement, "You cannot worship both God and money."

In many cases, money will not solve your problem. Over 51,000 families in America filed bankruptcy last year then hired a lawyer to get them out with the intention of non-payment. The issue of living paycheck to paycheck is not only a physical concern, but it is also a spiritual concern. The personal savings rate of our people is a negative 0.6%. This means that for every $100 we received, we spent $100.65 which means that the average household each month spends more than what comes in. We are slaughtering ourselves, committing financial suicide and don't even realize it.

I'm reminded of something George Patton said as a general in the Army of the United States. He was a great commander with a God-given insight into war and he knew how vital a winning attitude could be. When addressing his troops once, he put it this way: "Some of you men have come with your minds made up to die for our country. That's not the way to win a war! The way to win a war is to make your enemies die for theirs!" George Patton had his mind made up to win and he knew that dying wasn't the way to do it. He had a winning attitude and so did I when I found myself sinking in a never-ending financial deficit.

You have a better reason to have a winning attitude than George Patton. God has guaranteed your success in everything you attempt to accomplish. Imagine you're about to tackle a tough job. And before you even get started on it, God speaks to you right out loud and says, "I just want you to know, I'm going to personally see to it that this project you're working on succeeds." Wouldn't that give you a tremendous feeling of confidence? Even if you ran into some rough spots, you wouldn't worry about failing because you had God's word that you were going to succeed.

God said in his Word that you're an "Overcomer!" In him, you can overcome any problem the world throws your way. It doesn't matter how much you feel like a loser. It doesn't matter how many times you've failed in the past. If you believe that Jesus is the Christ, the Son of the Living God then you've committed yourself to overcoming the world. You've been given the power to do it.

If you believe the Word of God then you should respond to every challenge by saying, "Well, praise God, I'm an overcomer!" Does having that attitude guarantee you won't have any trouble? No! It simply means you can go through that trouble and emerge triumphantly. Jesus said, "These things I have spoken unto you, that in me ye might have peace. In the world ye shall have tribulation: but be of good cheer; I have overcome the world." In other words, Jesus is saying, "The world will come at you with every thing it has to offer, but don't you worry about it—I've already beat it—I've already overcome the world."

The Church, the Body of Christ, has lived far below her privileges. We have lived as far below our spiritual privileges as Israel has lived below her political privileges. Israel should be the head and not the tail by now. She should not have to borrow from any nation on earth and every nation on earth should be in debt to her. Well, that's how far below our spiritual privileges the Body of Christ has lived.

Down through the years, God exercised his faith for us. He was willing to work for over 2,000 years to get his plan functioning properly. The whole time the world laid in darkness, God was still believing and still exercising faith in you and I that we no longer be carried away by foolishness. He had to believe that you and I would supply what it took to hold the Body together. We failed and we failed and we failed again, but God kept on joining and believing. He never uttered words of failure. Theology cried, "The Church is failing!" God said, "My house will be full and the gates of hell will not prevail against it!" Religion was failing—God wasn't! Can't you see his attitude?

You can't afford to think as a loser. Change your attitude. The whole Body of Christ is counting on you. You're one with him in the Spirit, you have the mind of Christ, you are bone of his bone, so you may as well be attitude of his attitude! He sees you as an overcomer, so you need to see yourself that way too!

One time the Lord showed me a vision of a man holding a big banana. The man began to peel the banana, and as he did, I saw that there was no banana inside, but standing in the bottom was a little man. That little man was me! The Lord said, "Son, that's your attitude toward yourself." It was true. I presented a big front to the world, but actually felt very small on the inside. The Lord told me I needed to change my entire attitude, so I did.

He began to show me from his Word what it meant to be in Christ and to have him in me. I began to see that a born-again believer is a limitless creature of God, an unlimited powerhouse of the very life of God himself. You need to realize this in your life. Allow God to supernaturally change your attitude. Allow him to reveal himself to you and give you this winning attitude to succeed in everything you attempt.

When a farmer puts a seed in the ground, he does not get back just one seed. He puts that seed into the earth, the seed produces a stalk of corn, the stalk produces an ear of corn, and the ear produces hundreds of new seeds—all from one seed the farmer planted! That's verification that God is able to give you everything you need and more.

Many people are beginning to catch the vision of being bankers for God. They have learned that they cannot give too much away when giving in the name of the Lord. Each time they give to enhance the will of God, he uses it for his purposes and returns it multiplied to them in greater abundance. The cycle continues to grow because we cannot out-give God no matter how hard we try.

During these times of economic chaos and unpredictable money markets, these "Spiritual bankers" have found the secret to God's abundance, and they now bank on God, bank on his promises and look to no other earthly bank for their source. By now the

Spirit of God is already working on you. I believe God wants you to know and understand his biblical principles and begin applying them. In fact, he cannot bless you financially until, by your gift, you first release him to act on your behalf.

This release process applies not only to money, but to any area of your life. Every day, spiritual forces of faith and fear fight on the battlefield of your mind and spirit. You are constantly faced with decisions to trust God and his promises in faith, or to function in fear apart from his promises. Every day you make a choice: either you exercise faith and feast in the abundance of God's supply, or you give in to the devil and fear, and suffer a personal famine.

God's servant Isaac fought the same battle. There was a famine in his land. The ground was dry. Isaac had a need, but there was no answer in sight. Fearful he would starve if he stayed in Israel, Isaac decided to go into Egypt to avoid the famine.

In this situation, Egypt and Israel are symbolic for your life. Egypt stood for the world and man's ability. Israel stood for God and his ability—his supply. God warned Isaac not to go into Egypt! In fact, God instructed Isaac to not only stay in the land, but he commanded him to sow in the midst of the famine, hunger and drought.

Isaac had to make a decision. He could ignore God, give in to his fear, see only the circumstances of drought and famine, or he could see beyond his condition, exercise faith and be obedient to God. He chose to stay in the land and sow. He chose faith and obedience to God's promises over fear. Do you know that before God prospered Isaac, Isaac had to do one more thing? He had to put his faith into action and sow seeds—precious sacrificial seeds. Never are seeds more precious and valuable than in a time of famine, a time of personal needs, especially when children are included in the equation.

Raising a child from birth through age 18 will cost a typical middle-income family almost $235,000 according to a report released from the United States Department of Agriculture. It's important you start planning early for their exit into the real world. However, saving for your own retirement should take priority over saving for your child's college education. Student loans and part-time jobs abound for the college crowd, but loans generally cannot be used for retirement. The average cost of tuition and fees for the 2013-2014 school year is approximately $8,544 for a public college and $31,700 for a private one with a yearly increase. Parents who want to chip in may consider setting aside some money today in a tax-advantaged 529 college savings plan.

There are first-time parent considerations to every budget prior to the child's birth. Long before the due date, examine how your baby will affect everyday expenses, including pricing life insurance policies, just in case there are complications during or after the pregnancy. Stroll through baby stores, take notes and then recreate your annual budget to include the new line items. This exercise can help you figure out if you need to cut spending in other areas. If one parent is thinking about leaving the workplace to care for the baby at home, try living on one income, well before the baby arrives, to see how feasible it is.

Your child won't know the difference between top-of-the-line baby blankets and less expensive quality ones that feel just as snuggly. Hand-me-downs, consignment shops, garage sales and even eBay are great sources for gently used-quality children clothes at bargain prices. These are all helpful tips to assist parents in retaining funds for a much needed use later on!

Parents are committed to teach and demonstrate proper stewardship as their children grows-up and increase in age. Children learn a lot from their parents financial habits, often by example. Teaching your children to work for their money in a fun way is a smart idea. You should perhaps connect their allowance with tasks related to various careers. This way, the child is making the connection between effort and money attained through employment. A perpetual generation will suffer tremendously in all areas if parents fail in their presentation.

After managing over 1.5 million dollars of government revenues in the United States Naval Armed Forces, I can honestly attest that Americans love spending money. Advertisers reinforce easy and insidious ideas to entice people to spend their money—NOW! Consumer reports state nearly every household in this country has a minimum of $9,200 in credit card debt, but excessive spending can make it difficult to achieve your long-term financial goal. There's nothing wrong with spending your hard earned money, if you prioritize it appropriately.

God call's a person who will not return his initial money to him at the local church assembly, through tithe and offering, a "Robber." With multiple locks on doors and fancy alarm systems around the premises, a "Robber" disguises themselves as a friend for an entrance. They're never concerned about locked doors or alarm codes. They've mastered the usage of advanced technology, but are unaware that their picture is posted in an all-points bulletin (APB) in heaven at the courthouse. If you want God to start blessing you abundantly, start giving him what's right—as opposed to what's left.

God is excited in the prosperity of his people. Would it be inaccurate to state that everyone: attending church services, clapping their hands, patting their feet to the sounds of the music and boosting the preacher with a host of "Amen" salutations, are not all God's people? Jesus said, "You are my friends, if you do what I command you."

The devil doesn't want you blessed, the windows in heaven opened for you or success to wholly come in your direction. If you've noticed; he does everything in his ability to convince you to go against God's plan so he may retain dominion and power over your progress. He delights in you living in bondage and his gates preventing you from reaching your full potential of existence. As long as you disregard the journey God is leading you, the farther you will find yourself from your true purpose. To show your friendship to God and prevent further separation from him, you should make an impressive attempt in following the clear teachings of Jesus Christ.

Now is the time to take your eyes off your circumstances. If you are in a famine, take your eyes off your fears. Put your faith into action and sow in your time of famine. God is faithful and as you render services to him then he will multiply your actions back to you. God wants to make a mighty witness of your faithfulness, just as he did with Isaac.

The world teaches, "Hide your treasures because times are hard. Get all you can, can all you get and then guard the can." The Word of God teaches, "They that sow in tears shall reap in joy." When do you sow in tears? When the seed is precious and when the times are hard! These are not my words or my ideas; they are from the Word of God. You can bank on his promises because I have. I even cast some bread on the water in the form of money and in return, along with the primary quantity, found interest dividends.

The taboo topic of getting by is not God's will for your life. Several people have the audacity to think God is angry at them when they're blessed. Their neighbors or family members may be angry, but it's exciting to God when they're blessed because it brings with it a praise report for public consideration. I decree that you will not be broke or live paycheck to paycheck another season of your life after the purchase of this book, sowing into this ministry and adhering to the financial freedom plan in its entirety. Stewardship is a matter of the heart!

Jesus Christ addressed this point through observation at a church service as he sat opposite the treasury and saw how the people placed their money in the designated container. He intentionally evaluated the offertory period to retrieve a vivid picture of the people hearts who contributed at this rich worship experience. As several individuals brought large and massive monetary contributions, a poor widow-lady gave all the money she possessed. This lady's giving, in terms of percentage, was much greater than the preceding givers amount collectively.

"Trusting God to supply all your needs according to his riches in glory" is difficult for a number of people. I keep asking myself, in spite of others, "What more can I give unto the Lord for all he's done for me?" He restored my health from a 2011 stroke, paralysis and impending amputation of my legs. It was no one but God who healed and restored the blood circulation deficiency in my entire body within 48 hours of my medical doctor's diagnosis. "What shall I give unto the Lord for all his benefits toward me?"

Once again, we see God's ways are not the ways of man. It seems only natural that if you were faithful in spiritual matters then God would trust you with money and wealth. The motto on our coins and money in the United States is, "In God We Trust." Have you ever thought that the reverse is also true? "In You God Trust." You must first be faithful with your money before God will trust you with spiritual matters.

When the eyes of your understanding are opened in the spiritual realm to glimpse your increase in the natural, you'll cease comfort in living paycheck to paycheck. Dirty giving is normally stemmed from brain cells triggered and transported by one's giving stance from a dirty heart. It's only when individuals gain a copious righteous heart that their giving is pleasing to God because "So as a man thinks in his heart, so is he."

If you never believe in the full gospel, you will forever live in degradation and forfeit God's promises of acquiring you "Good measures, pressed down, shaken together and running over" of substance from other blessed individuals. Your receiving depends on the manner of your giving. If you give grudgingly, you will receive grudgingly! God has given his best and requires from us not anything less.

We all make mistakes, especially when pertaining to finances, but is it really fair that we should have to spend the rest of our lives paying for it? If you don't have time to get it right now, when will you have time to fix it? God wants you to prosper and be in good health, but you cannot prosper in every dimension of your life living paycheck to paycheck. When God thinks of your specific name in conjunction with the time, talent and treasures you've contributed toward your future; you should want him to remember the promises he made to you and without any questions or reservations, go ahead and open up the windows of heaven, pouring out abundant blessings in your direction.

It's your giving that lubricates the window hinges in heaven for the purpose of God distributing good things to you and your family. He doesn't only sign your paycheck, he is in charge of all promotions and he won't ever take you where his grace won't protect you. If God can't trust you to give him back $1 out of $10 then what make you think he can trust your hands with $100? As stewards, you must understand the path to financial freedom. "God has raised us up together and made us sit together in heavenly places in Christ Jesus," but several people are only sightseeing now because they spent their extra along the way. Start hearing God's voice and obey it at all times.

CHAPTER ELEVEN

How To Get Your Hands Out The Lion Mouth

By now, you are well aware that this is not the usual Christian book. We have explored some shocking and tradition-shattering ideas about giving, receiving and money. In this chapter, the shock of God's word will continue to shake your spirit and help you retrieve your hands from the mouth of this deadly beast that's causing your financial demise.

Well, Skeptic, sit back and recite these words with me:

"But thou shalt remember the Lord thy God: for it is he that giveth thee power to get wealth, that he may establish his covenant which he sware unto thy fathers, as it is this day."

Once again we have a controversial idea—God gives you the power to attain wealth. The idea is not mine! If you have any problems with this concept, please seek the Lord because I did in 2002. It was as clear as day and I was exhausted from deficit battling when God opened my eyes of understanding to reveal a gift that would soon gain me wealth, giving me the ability and strength to extract my hands from the lion mouth. Yes, the gift of writing! I learned and matured the gift, as a Master Training Specialist, in the United States Navy. To my surprise: my first book published, "How To Save Your Marriage Without Losing Your Mind," was my ticket and means out of deficit along with adhering to a strict conducive financial plan and personal budgeting technique that fit my income status.

The bible says, "God is the one who gives you the power to get wealth." Any skill, trade, profession, vocation or anything that helps you to earn income, that ability comes from God and is awaiting your use. So often we are taught that when we have a spiritual problem, we go to the Lord. But he cares not only about your spirit: he cares about all of you. If you have a desire to increase your potential to earn income then seek the Lord. Ask him where you should go to improve your skills. What better employment counselor could you have than the great God of heaven?

". . . it is he that giveth thee power to get wealth . . ."

In the natural, that sounds almost like a vulgar and ridiculous concept. In the spiritual, when you see your Father as someone who cares about all aspects of your life—even the financial—it becomes just another compliment to the giving, loving and concerned nature of our Creator. Two of the names given to him in the bible are, "The Mighty God" and "Counselor." So you really think God would ask you to give something in the form of tithes and offerings to him that he did not give you the ability to get? Of course not! Do you think God would put it on your heart to give $100 or $1,000 to a gospel project and then not give you the means to honor that pledge? Of course not!

I believe God does burden your heart to give to a certain project and I believe God does provide you with the ability to honor that pledge. Whenever I am in a revival crusade or any place where there is a challenge to reach lost souls, I want to get involved with the money God entrusted to my stewardship. God has never let me down and each time I make a pledge for his work, he gives me the ability to meet the pledge.

The Lord not only directs what you are to give, but he also provides you the ability to receive. He has in his hands and power, the ability to prosper you, to speak to you and guide you as you become more and more obedient to his will. When God gives you a burden to do something, the very God of heaven can also bring it to pass because it is he who gives you the power to get wealth. The skill is in your hands and the ability is in your mind, but the power is from God.

The special talent you have, whatever it is, has been given to you by God and the proceeds from a portion of that talent should be used to further the kingdom of God here on earth. God wants to lead you: let go and let him. In prayer, ask him where he wants you to go and then listen for his guidance. Who knows better than God where to lead you to accomplish your task in this season?

Years ago Evangelist Oral Roberts used to say at the close of each of his broadcasts, "Something good is going to happen to you!" Some Christians became upset with him for making that statement. "How does he know that something good is going to happen to me?" they asked. "He doesn't even know me." Of course, the answer is that Oral Roberts wasn't talking to them. He was talking to those who prayed, believed and fully expected God to answer their prayers, to intervene in their situation and to do something marvelous about it. He knew that his God would hear and answer prayer on his people behalf.

In the natural, things are not looking good. Businesses and industries are experiencing financial difficulties and are reducing costs and overheard wherever they can. Workers are being laid off. Jobs are being eliminated. The unemployment rate, although sometimes improving, has increased dramatically. Banks and savings and loan institutions are failing. Bankruptcies are rampant. Inflation is again on the rise. The national debt is skyrocketing out of control. Economic unrest and instability are having an adverse effect on every area of our lives internationally.

Faced with that kind of depressing economic situation, you and I have no choice but to get on God's system because it is the only system that is working. That's why I urge people to get on it now and not wait until the famine has struck with full force. If things look bad now and you think the world's system is failing at this point; you haven't seen anything yet. The entire system is crumbling. It is all falling apart. It is being torn down bit by bit. It will soon get to the place that no one can trust anything man builds.

When that happens, only those who are on God's system will be able to stand head and shoulders about the crowd and say, "Our God supplies all our needs according to his riches in glory in Christ Jesus." So once you hear the Word of God, don't lean on the arm of flesh. God is abundance minded. He is not interested in meeting our immediate needs; he also wants us to have enough leftover to live on for years to come.

For most people, following basic money rules makes sense. But like everything else in life, there are situations when following tried-and-true advice might not work. Professional financial managers weigh-in on when to consider the exceptions. Saving enough money to pay three to six months of living expenses will lessen the chances you'll have to sell assets and go into debt in case of an unexpected big-ticket expense or job loss. Building your emergency fund in something safe and liquid, such as a savings account, should be a top priority along with paying down any high-interest consumer debt.

If your debt is of the low-rate, tax-reducing variety, such as a mortgage or student loans, and your retirement plan at work offers a match, you might be better off contributing enough to receive the full company match before focusing on building your emergency fund and eliminating debt. Remember that contributions to a traditional employer-sponsored retirement account such as a 401(k) or Thrift Savings Plan may reduce your tax bill. When viable, add the money from your employer match and you've got a hard-to-beat combination. If you don't participate in these plans, you could be missing out on valuable benefits and tax savings.

Contributing at least $1 to your savings (or 401(k) or TSP) for every $10 you earn or 10% is an old rule of thumb, will help you in the long run. And it's certainly better than 3.6%, which is the current national savings rate, according to the Commerce Department. If you didn't begin saving for retirement until you were in your 30's or older, it may take more effort to achieve your retirement goal. A late start means you've probably got ground to make-up and 10% is probably not enough to close the gap. If you need to increase your retirement savings and are not already contributing the maximum amount allowed to your 401(k), a reasonable reaction is to immediately boost your contribution rate.

To create a better tax-management plan, you may need to look beyond your employer's plan. If you don't have a Roth 401(k) available, you may be better off contributing just enough to take full advantage of a match (if your employer offers one), but then sending additional savings to a Roth IRA, if you're eligible. A Roth contribution won't lower your tax bill today, but the possibility of qualified tax-free withdrawals during retirement is a benefit. You'll likely have control over future income tax bills by having money in pretax and Roth accounts.

The average college graduate earns $26,618 more a year than someone with just a high school education. As a result, most financial planners agree that helping your child get a college education is important. To avoid overpaying for a diploma, look for cost-effective ways to get an education, such as spending the first two years at a community college, then transferring to a four-year college. If helping pay for your child's four-year college degree places an extreme burden and strain on your finances, you should consider other, more affordable ways to accomplish this goal as mentioned previously. The return depends on the price you pay and where that money comes from.

You should consider buying a house if the cost of rent is 2.5 times your annual income or less. This is a reasonable guide when determining whether you can afford to buy a home. If it doesn't suit your circumstances, disregard this guideline. However, "Why spend your hard-earned money purchasing a home for your landlord when you can buy one for yourself?" What really matters is whether you can afford the monthly payment, factoring in taxes, insurance, maintenance, current mortgage rates and the size of your down payment including the closing cost. Plus, consider how long you'll live in the house. If you plan to move in a few years, renting may be the better decision.

Historically speaking, the supposed 4% rule calls for a retiree to make annual inflation-adjusted withdrawals and be reasonably sure the portfolio will last 30 years. For most retirees, it's a fine starting point to determine how much they can spend. Your plan for retirement is not a smooth glide path. Retirees may prefer withdrawing more in good times and cutting back when times get tough or varying distributions based on their investment results. Also, adjustments should be made according to other sources of income. Some retirees may wish to withdraw more at first and delay taking Social Security, but then withdraw less once the Social Security benefit kicks in. Whatever your plan, it should be monitored and adjusted as necessary.

God will show you how to profit. Maybe even aide you in opening your own business. He will guide you, but you must listen and follow his instructions attentively as he gives you peace like a river in the midst of adversities. In the translation of the Hebrew language, the word peace is "Shalom." It means well-being, health and prosperity. God wants to teach you how to be healthy and how to prosper. As you stay on his course, in his will and obey his command; he'll be the best partner you've ever had.

Let him lead you! Let him guide you! And when you have reached the end of your rope, listen to him because, "Blessed is the man that walketh not in the counsel of the ungodly, nor standeth in the way of sinners, nor sitteth in the seat of the scornful. But his delight is in the law of the Lord; and in his law doth he meditate day and night. And he shall be like a tree planted by the rivers of water, that bringeth forth his fruit in his season; his leaf also shall not wither; and whatsoever he doeth shall prosper."

The Lord's methodical way of operating is precisely opposite of the world's stimulus. The biblical laws of sowing shatter many traditional thoughts and often send even faithful Christians back to their bibles in panic, anxiously turning pages. Like the Skeptic, they pray: "Lord, say it isn't so. That means I will have to change my mind, to readjust my way of thinking!" In the zone of the spirit, the Bible's truth can often be painful. But praise God, through his grace and guidance all things can be overcome.

Economist everywhere encourage their investors to grab up every piece of property, buy up all the gold and silver, get greater percentage of a corporation's stock and then hold it. These investment portfolios are a hypothetical source of security in these troubled times, but look what is happening even in the natural monarchy. Property taxes and housing values have slowed from their previous fast pace. Gold prices have dropped in the last few years and silver investments were rocked over the hoarding by a few investors that caused value to drop drastically. Stock prices have been so up and down the past decade that many investors must be dizzy from the roller coaster ride. The ways of the world simply are not working.

God's word is founded in generosity. In the Old and New Testament scriptures the theory is the same: "As you are generous in all things, you will be prospered, fat, watered and blessed." This is not a sales gimmick invented by some ministry to get you to participate in giving, but this is God's guarantee, his Word and his promise. Generosity is a characteristic of God. When you are generous, it is God's personality beaming through you. As you sow liberally into God's field, he will see to it that you reap an abundant harvest for his glory.

In order to reap the harvest, every farmer needs to know the laws of nature concerning how to produce a crop. It's so true in the spiritual empire as well that you and I thoroughly understand the laws of sowing. God is not mocked! Each time I smile, I can expect to receive a smile in return. When I frown, I had better be prepared to see an ugly face. I always get back what I plant. God's principles do not change!

Adversity is normally the activator of our faith. God love us so much that he presents an antidote prescription for *all* illness. He said, "If my people who are called by my name, shall humble themselves, and pray, and seek my face, and turn from their wicked ways; then will I hear from heaven, and will forgive their sin, and will heal their land." When God is finished pruning you, you'll be similar to a matured tree planted by the rivers of water, bringing forth good and ripe fruit in your season.

Everyone in our society has different seasons so don't get deterrent, irritable or bent out of shape when God blesses others in your surrounding area prior to blessing you. If you remain fixed, focused and faithful, in due time, your turn will come. God will never plant you in a place where you will not grow. Your lack of growth brings no glory to him. It simply violates God's very own doctrine of creation. In the process of creating you, he purposely intended you to meet your destiny.

If you are not growing as fast as you desire; it may be you've replanted yourself, rather than, allowing God to mature you on the fertile soil near the rivers of waters he initially planted you. Each tree must be planted in the right soil temperature, in the right depth and in the right season. You may want to ask yourself the question: "Am I really where God intended me to be for his glory to retrieve the best from me?"

The uniqueness concerning roots is that they will attach themselves to anything that's in their growing path. I have learned from experience as a homeowner that whether sidewalks or pipes underground, roots will attach itself to it. Be very careful of the people you associate and partner with because as the cliché affirm, "Birds of a feather flock together."

The overlook of these truthful facts have caused numerous people to suffer from staunch of growth, never reaching their full potential, living beneath God's plan and buried below their divine purpose. People that tell you for no reason, "Don't forget where you came from" are mad because they're still there, rooted in terrible soil, entangled around bad attitudes, congested by hellish spirits and diffused by non-effective traditions. As a people, we will never succeed through mediocrity, foolishness or comfort, unless we seize faithfulness and conversion given to us by the truth.

In our current era, debt has to be the greatest cause of depression. A limited amount of people are labeled as debt-free. The world is calling upon you for debt consolidation, but what you really need is unnecessary debt elimination. Debt can be compared metaphorically to a lion, making the entire process quite tricky. If your hands are so far in his mouth that you are unable to view your fingernails or in debt to the point you can't contribute cheerfully and regularly to the support of the ministry; you should set in motion the financial freedom plan, terminating all debt and thereafter, establish an emergency and reserve fund.

If you want to remove your hands from the lion mouth, you must start controlling your finances, instead of your finances controlling you. Unless you were taught very early in life, many people figure since they have money, why not spend it. This state of mind has gotten a whole lot of individuals in a world of trouble. When you run out of substance, resources and financial security, you start borrowing what you can't payback and charging amounts you don't have at the moment.

It's tempting to take banks and credit card companies up on their pre-approval offers, but the problem is, they don't always factor in your future income changes. Forgetting to look beyond the numbers may be a hindrance for you later. You might be able to financially afford to buy it now, but is it worth it to you? Your lifestyle, cost of living increase and personal preferences all play a vital role in deciding whether it makes sense to purchase unnecessary items. Living a life perpetrating that of the "So-Called Joneses" will not permit maneuvering in a closely controlled system.

You must learn to save more than you spend. We live in a consumer generation that makes everything attractive, but you have to ignore the fancy sounds of the siren. Just because you make on average $300 weekly, doesn't necessary mean you have to spend the entire $300 weekly. At some point, you should become tired of being defeated and hunger for better. You are buying too much and too expensive, when you should be aiming to save earlier in terms of your age. I promote waiting for the sale to go on and never be in such a hurry or too excited to get it because you may be disappointed in the end.

It's essential you launch goals toward completing your financial egress. If bill collectors are ringing your phone frequently then that's evident you are in jeopardy, but never stop sowing.

Don't stop giving just because the conditions necessary for planting and reaping looks unfavorable. Remember the agricultural and spiritual law that we have already set forth. When in a famine, don't eat that last bit of seed, but sow it in hope and earnest expectation of a multiplied harvest. The bible says, "The wealth of the sinner is laid up for the just." Eventually, all that wealth will come into our hands and the world will be envious of us. But that will only happen when we learn to appropriate the laws of God.

Do you realize that if people won't listen, God can speak to the birds of the air and command them to feed you? Every time a bird flies over my house, I ask, "Is he the one, Lord?" Every time an old dog comes by and starts to dig up my yard, I say, "Go to it, boy; dig, dig, dig." Katherine screams, "Get that mutt out of there, he's digging up my flowers!" But I answer, "Leave him alone. God said that the hidden riches belong to me. That old dog may come up with some of them." Every time I go fishing and reel in a catch, I open the fish's mouth and look inside to see if there is any tax money in there. I don't want to take any chances on missing out on God's miracle provision.

Now you may be thinking, "Henry Armington, you are a nut!" I may be, but I am a happy, healthy, successful and prosperous nut. I believe that is because I do as the men and women of the Bible, and put my faith and trust in the Lord and not in man. That kind of material provision is as much as part of the heritage of the Saints of the Lord, as salvation of our souls and divine health is for our physical bodies.

God is always a step ahead of any event that may arise to avert you from succeeding. He is always ahead of a bad economy, a step ahead of unemployment, a pace ahead of a famine, a stride ahead of recession and a march ahead of depression. If you position your faith and trust in him and remain obedient to his word, he will command his blessings upon you, regardless of your situation or circumstances. He will turn your crisis into triumphs, every stumbling block into stepping stones and every curse into a blessing. That, too, is the heritage of the Saints of the Lord.

God has plans for your life. He has a purpose for your existence. He has victories for you yet to achieve. To reach your life-long goals, you must have a great and positive spirit of anticipation and enough conviction to turn your adversities into victories. "Perseverance must finish its work so that you may be mature and complete, not lacking anything." I encourage you now, with the material provided for your enhancement, to write your next chapter toward an optimistic finale in joining the Elite.

SCRIPTURE REFERENCES

CHAPTER ONE

John 1:23 He said, I am the voice of one crying in the wilderness, Make straight the way of the Lord, as said the prophet Esaias.

Philippians 2:9 Wherefore God also hath highly exalted him, and given him a name which is above every name: that at the name of Jesus every knee should bow, of things in heaven, and things in earth, and things under the earth; and that every tongue should confess that Jesus Christ is Lord, to the glory of God the Father.

Luke 3:15-20 And as the people were in expectation, and all men mused in their hearts of John, whether he were the Christ, or not; John answered, saying unto them all, I indeed baptize you with water; but one mightier than I cometh, the latchet of whose shoes I am not worthy to unloose: he shall baptize you with the Holy Ghost and with fire: Whose fan is in his hand, and he will throughly purge his floor, and will gather the wheat into his garner; but the chaff he will burn with fire unquenchable. And many other things in his exhortation preached he unto the people. But Herod the tetrarch, being reproved by him for Herodias his brother Philip's wife, and for all the evils which Herod had done, Added yet this above all, that he shut up John in prison.

John 1:29 The next day John seeth Jesus coming unto him, and saith, Behold the Lamb of God, which taketh away the sin of the world.

Matthew 5:16 Let your light so shine before men, that they may see your good works, and glorify your Father which is in heaven.

CHAPTER TWO

Joshua 2:10 For we have heard how the LORD dried up the water of the Red sea for you, when ye came out of Egypt; and what ye did unto the two kings of the Amorites, that were on the other side Jordan, Sihon and Og, whom ye utterly destroyed.

1 Corinthians 10:2-5 And were all baptized unto Moses in the cloud and in the sea; And did all eat the same spiritual meat; And did all drink the same spiritual drink: for they drank of that spiritual Rock that followed them: and that Rock was Christ. But with many of them God was not well pleased: for they were overthrown in the wilderness.

Romans 6:3-7 Know ye not, that so many of us as were baptized into Jesus Christ were baptized into his death? Therefore we are buried with him by baptism into death: that like as Christ was raised up from the dead by the glory of the Father, even so we also should walk in newness of life. For if we have been planted together in the likeness of his death, we shall be also in the likeness of his resurrection: Knowing this, that our old man is crucified with him, that the body of sin might be destroyed, that henceforth we should not serve sin. For he that is dead is freed from sin.

1 Peter 1:22 Seeing ye have purified your souls in obeying the truth through the Spirit unto unfeigned love of the brethren, see that ye love one another with a pure heart fervently.

CHAPTER THREE

Psalm 37:24 Though he fall, he shall not be utterly cast down: for the LORD upholdeth him with his hand.

James 2:17 Even so faith, if it hath not works, is dead, being alone.

John 10:10 The thief cometh not, but for to steal, and to kill, and to destroy: I am come that they might have life, and that they might have it more abundantly.

Hebrews 11:1 Now faith is the substance of things hoped for, the evidence of things not seen.

Philippians 3:13 Brethren, I count not myself to have apprehended: but this one thing I do, forgetting those things which are behind, and reaching forth unto those things which are before.

1 John 2:17 And the world passeth away, and the lust thereof: but he that doeth the will of God abideth for ever.

Romans 10:9 That if thou shalt confess with thy mouth the Lord Jesus, and shalt believe in thine heart that God hath raised him from the dead, thou shalt be saved.

CHAPTER FOUR

1 John 4:4 Ye are of God, little children, and have overcome them: because greater is he that is in you, than he that is in the world.

Mark 4:35 And the same day, when the even was come, he saith unto them, let us pass over unto the other side.

Hebrews 13:2 Be not forgetful to entertain strangers: for thereby some have entertained angels unawares.

Romans 12:10-13 Be kindly affectioned one to another with brotherly love; in honour preferring one another; not slothful in business; fervent in spirit; serving the Lord; rejoicing in hope; patient in tribulation; continuing instant in prayer; distributing to the necessity of saints; given to hospitality.

Romans 7:21 I find then a law, that, when I would do good, evil is present with me.

Job 1:7 And the Lord said unto Satan, whence comest thou? Then Satan answered the Lord, and said, from going to and fro in the earth, and from walking up and down in it.

Romans 7:24-25 O wretched man that I am! Who shall deliver me from the body of this death? I thank God through Jesus Christ our Lord. So then with the mind I myself serve the law of God; but with the flesh the law of sin.

CHAPTER FIVE

Habakkuk 1:2 O Lord, how long shall I cry, and thou wilt not hear! Even cry out unto thee of violence, and thou wilt not save!

Psalm 90:12 So teach us to number our days, that we may apply our hearts unto wisdom.

Isaiah 54:17 No weapon that is formed against thee shall prosper; and every tongue that shall rise against thee in judgment thou shalt condemn. This is the heritage of the servants of the Lord, and their righteousness is of me, saith the Lord.

Deuteronomy 28:13 And the Lord shall make thee the head, and not the tail; and thou shalt be above only, and thou shalt not be beneath; if that thou hearken unto the commandments of the Lord thy God, which I command thee this day, to observe and to do them.

Proverbs 22:7 The rich ruleth over the poor, and the borrower is servant to the lender.

1 John 4:4 Ye are of God, little children, and have overcome them: because greater is he that is in you, than he that is in the world.

Proverbs 28:18 Whoso walketh uprightly shall be saved: but he that is perverse in his ways shall fall at once.

1 Corinthians 10:13 There hath no temptation taken you but such as is common to man: but God is faithful, who will not suffer you to be tempted above that ye are able; but will with the temptation also make a way to escape, that ye may be able to bear it.

CHAPTER SIX

Acts 5:1-8 But a certain man named Ananias, with Sapphira his wife, sold a possession, and kept back part of the price, his wife also being privy to it, and brought a certain part, and laid it at the apostles' feet. But Peter said, Ananias, Why hath Satan filled thine heart to lie to the Holy Ghost, and to keep back part of the price of the land? Whiles it remained, was it not thine own? And after it was sold, was it not in thine own power? Why hast thou conceived this thing in thine heart? Thou hast not lied unto men, but unto God. And Ananias hearing these words fell down, and gave up the ghost: and great fear came on all them that heard these things. And the young men arose, wound him up, and carried him out, and buried him. And it was about the space of three hours after, when his wife, not knowing what was done, came in. And Peter answered unto her, Tell me whether ye sold the land for so much? And she said, Yea, for so much.

Psalm 118:24-25 This is the day which the LORD hath made; we will rejoice and be glad in it. Save now, I beseech thee, O LORD: O LORD, I beseech thee, send now prosperity.

Romans 6:23 For the wages of sin is death; but the gift of God is eternal life through Jesus Christ our Lord.

2 Corinthians 12:7 And lest I should be exalted above measure through the abundance of the revelations, there was given to me a thorn in the flesh, the messenger of Satan to buffet me, lest I should be exalted above measure.

CHAPTER SEVEN

Exodus 14:5-22 And it was told the king of Egypt that the people fled: and the heart of Pharaoh and of his servants was turned against the people, and they said, Why have we done this, that we have let Israel go from serving us? And he made ready his chariot, and took his people with him: and he took six hundred chosen chariots, and all the chariots of Egypt, and captains over every one of them. And the LORD hardened the heart of Pharaoh king of Egypt, and he pursued after the children of Israel: and the children of Israel went out with an high hand. But the Egyptians pursued after them, all the horses and chariots of Pharaoh, and his horsemen, and his army, and overtook them encamping by the sea, beside Pihahiroth, before Baalzephon. And when Pharaoh drew nigh, the children of Israel lifted up their eyes, and, behold, the Egyptians marched after them; and they were sore afraid: and the children of Israel cried out unto the LORD. And they said unto Moses, Because there were no graves in Egypt, hast thou taken us away to die in the wilderness? Wherefore hast thou dealt thus with us, to carry us forth out of Egypt? Is not this the word that we did tell thee in Egypt, saying, Let us alone, that we may serve the Egyptians? For it had been better for us to serve the Egyptians, than that we should die in the wilderness. And Moses said unto the people, Fear ye not, stand still, and see the salvation of the LORD, which he will shew to you to day: for the Egyptians whom ye have seen to day, ye shall see them again no more for ever. The LORD shall fight for you, and ye shall hold your peace. And the LORD said unto Moses, Wherefore criest thou unto me? Speak unto the children of Israel, that they go forward: but lift thou up thy rod, and stretch out thine hand over the sea, and divide it: and the children of Israel shall go on dry ground through the midst of the sea. And I, behold, I will harden the hearts of the Egyptians, and they shall follow them: and I will get me honour upon Pharaoh, and upon all his host, upon his chariots, and upon his horsemen. And the Egyptians shall know that I am the LORD, when I have gotten me honour upon Pharaoh, upon his chariots, and upon his horsemen. And the angel of God, which went before the camp of Israel, removed and went behind them; and the pillar of the cloud went from before their face, and stood behind them: and it came between the camp of the Egyptians and the camp of Israel; and it was a cloud and darkness to them, but it gave light by night to these: so that the one came not near the other all the night. And Moses stretched out his hand over the sea; and the LORD caused the sea to go back by a strong east wind all that night, and made the sea dry land, and the waters were divided. And the children of Israel went into the midst of the sea upon the dry ground: and the waters were a wall unto them on their right hand, and on their left.

Matthew 6:33 But seek ye first the kingdom of God, and his righteousness; and all these things shall be added unto you.

Exodus 1:10 Come on, let us deal wisely with them; lest they multiply, and it come to pass, that, when there falleth out any war, they join also unto our enemies, and fight against us, and so get them up out of the land.

Jeremiah 4:7 The lion is come up from his thicket, and the destroyer of the Gentiles is on his way; he is gone forth from his place to make thy land desolate; and thy cities shall be laid waste, without an inhabitant.

Isaiah 55:8 For my thoughts are not your thoughts, neither are your ways my ways, saith the LORD.

Psalm 23:4 Yea, though I walk through the valley of the shadow of death, I will fear no evil: for thou art with me; thy rod and thy staff they comfort me.

CHAPTER EIGHT

2 Samuel 16:5-13 And when king David came to Bahurim, behold, thence came out a man of the family of the house of Saul, whose name was Shimei, the son of Gera: he came forth, and cursed still as he came. And he cast stones at David, and at all the servants of king David: and all the people and all the mighty men were

on his right hand and on his left. And thus said Shimei when he cursed, Come out, come out, thou bloody man, and thou man of Belial: The LORD hath returned upon thee all the blood of the house of Saul, in whose stead thou hast reigned; and the LORD hath delivered the kingdom into the hand of Absalom thy son: and, behold, thou art taken in thy mischief, because thou art a bloody man. Then said Abishai the son of Zeruiah unto the king, Why should this dead dog curse my lord the king? Let me go over, I pray thee, and take off his head. And the king said, What have I to do with you, ye sons of Zeruiah? So let him curse, because the LORD hath said unto him, Curse David. Who shall then say, Wherefore hast thou done so? And David said to Abishai, and to all his servants, Behold, my son, which came forth of my bowels, seeketh my life: how much more now may this Benjamite do it? Let him alone, and let him curse; for the LORD hath bidden him. It may be that the LORD will look on mine affliction, and that the LORD will requite me good for his cursing this day. And as David and his men went by the way, Shimei went along on the hill's side over against him, and cursed as he went, and threw stones at him, and cast dust.

Genesis 41:33-36 Now therefore let Pharaoh look out a man discreet and wise, and set him over the land of Egypt. Let Pharaoh do this, and let him appoint officers over the land, and take up the fifth part of the land of Egypt in the seven plenteous years. And let them gather all the food of those good years that come, and lay up corn under the hand of Pharaoh, and let them keep food in the cities. And that food shall be for store to the land against the seven years of famine, which shall be in the land of Egypt; that the land perish not through the famine.

Psalm 46:10 Be still, and know that I am God: I will be exalted among the heathen, I will be exalted in the earth.

CHAPTER NINE

Luke 8:53 And they laughed him to scorn, knowing that she was dead.

Mark 10:46-52 And they came to Jericho: and as he went out of Jericho with his disciples and a great number of people, blind Bartimaeus, the son of Timaeus, sat by the highway side begging. And when he heard that it was Jesus of Nazareth, he began to cry out, and say, Jesus, thou son of David, have mercy on me. And many charged him that he should hold his peace: but he cried the more a great deal, Thou son of David, have mercy on me. And Jesus stood still, and commanded him to be called. And they call the blind man, saying unto him, Be of good comfort, rise; he calleth thee. And he, casting away his garment, rose, and came to Jesus. And Jesus answered and said unto him, What wilt thou that I should do unto thee? The blind man said unto him, Lord, that I might receive my sight. And Jesus said unto him, Go thy way; thy faith hath made thee whole. And immediately he received his sight, and followed Jesus in the way.

CHAPTER TEN

1 John 5:1-5 Whosoever believeth that Jesus is the Christ is born of God: and every one that loveth him that begat loveth him also that is begotten of him. By this we know that we love the children of God, when we love God, and keep his commandments. For this is the love of God, that we keep his commandments: and his commandments are not grievous. For whatsoever is born of God overcometh the world: and this is the victory that overcometh the world, even our faith. Who is he that overcometh the world, but he that believeth that Jesus is the Son of God?

Romans 8:37 Nay, in all these things we are more than conquerors through him that loved us.

John 16:33 These things I have spoken unto you, that in me ye might have peace. In the world ye shall have tribulation: but be of good cheer; I have overcome the world.

Ephesians 4:14 That we henceforth be no more children, tossed to and fro, and carried about with every wind of doctrine, by the sleight of men, and cunning craftiness, whereby they lie in wait to deceive.

2 Corinthians 9:8 And God is able to make all grace abound toward you; that ye, always having all sufficiency in all things, may abound to every good work.

Mark 12:41-44 And Jesus sat over against the treasury, and beheld how the people cast money into the treasury: and many that were rich cast in much. And there came a certain poor widow, and she threw in two mites, which make a farthing. And he called unto him his disciples, and saith unto them, Verily I say unto you, That this poor widow hath cast more in, than all they which have cast into the treasury: for all they did cast in of their abundance; but she of her want did cast in all that she had, even all her living.

Genesis 16:12 And he will be a wild man; his hand will be against every man, and every man's hand against him; and he shall dwell in the presence of all his brethren.

Malachi 3:8 Will a man rob God? Yet ye have robbed me. But ye say, Wherein have we robbed thee? In tithes and offerings.

Psalm 35:27 Let them shout for joy, and be glad, that favour my righteous cause: yea, let them say continually, Let the LORD be magnified, which hath pleasure in the prosperity of his servant.

Psalm 126:5 They that sow in tears shall reap in joy.

Ecclesiastes 11:1 Cast thy bread upon the waters: for thou shalt find it after many days.

Psalm 116:12 What shall I render unto the LORD for all his benefits toward me?

Proverbs 23:7 For as he thinketh in his heart, so is he: Eat and drink, saith he to thee; but his heart is not with thee.

Ephesians 2:6 And hath raised us up together, and made us sit together in heavenly places in Christ Jesus.

CHAPTER ELEVEN

Deuteronomy 8:18 But thou shalt remember the LORD thy God: for it is he that giveth thee power to get wealth, that he may establish his covenant which he sware unto thy fathers, as it is this day.

Philippians 4:19 But my God shall supply all your need according to his riches in glory by Christ Jesus.

Proverbs 11:24-25 There is that scattereth, and yet increaseth; and there is that withholdeth more than is meet, but it tendeth to poverty. The liberal soul shall be made fat: and he that watereth shall be watered also himself.

Psalm 1:1-3 Blessed is the man that walketh not in the counsel of the ungodly, nor standeth in the way of sinners, nor sitteth in the seat of the scornful. But his delight is in the law of the LORD; and in his law doth he meditate day and night. And he shall be like a tree planted by the rivers of water, that bringeth forth his fruit in his season; his leaf also shall not wither; and whatsoever he doeth shall prosper.

2 Chronicles 7:14 If my people, which are called by my name, shall humble themselves, and pray, and seek my face, and turn from their wicked ways; then will I hear from heaven, and will forgive their sin, and will heal their land.

1 Peter 5:8 Be sober, be vigilant; because your adversary the devil, as a roaring lion, walketh about, seeking whom he may devour.

Proverbs 13:22 A good man leaveth an inheritance to his children's children: and the wealth of the sinner is laid up for the just.

1 Kings 17:1-6 And Elijah the Tishbite, who was of the inhabitants of Gilead, said unto Ahab, As the LORD God of Israel liveth, before whom I stand, there shall not be dew nor rain these years, but according to my word. And the word of the LORD came unto him, saying, Get thee hence, and turn thee eastward, and hide thyself by the brook Cherith, that is before Jordan. And it shall be, that thou shalt drink of the brook; and I have commanded the ravens to feed thee there. So he went and did according unto the word of the LORD: for he went and dwelt by the brook Cherith, that is before Jordan. And the ravens brought him bread and flesh in the morning, and bread and flesh in the evening; and he drank of the brook.

FINANCIAL FREEDOM PLAN
WORKSHEETS

The following are sheets to assist you in achieving financial freedom.

However, if needing assistance, contact our staff for the next available workshop nearest you.

MONTHLY SPENDING RECORD

Keep track of your daily spending for two weeks consecutively. The secret is to record it when you spend it on a 30 day calendar designated for expenditures *ONLY*. Using a "stickee" note in your wallet or purse will help you track your spending until you are able to transfer each onto your designated calendar. When you go for your money, make a note on your "stickee"; (put the amount and what you spent your money on). At the end of the day, transfer the recorded amount to this report. Be sure to include bills paid, along with sodas, lunch, etc.

Sun	Mon	Tues	Wed	Thurs	Fri	Sat

Take Home Pay $ _____

Amount Spent $ _____

Balance $ _____

Sun	Mon	Tues	Wed	Thurs	Fri	Sat

Take Home Pay $ _____

Amount Spent $ _____

Balance $ _____

Note: Repeat steps for an additional two weeks and then forward information to the appropriate pages.

STATEMENT OF NET WORTH

ASSETS	LIABILITIES
Cash (on hand)	Signature Loans
Checking Accounts	Auto Loans or Lease
Savings Account	Consolidated Loan
Certificate of Deposit	Student Loan
Cash Value of Life Insurance	Dept Store Card
U.S. Saving Bonds	Credit Card
Mutual Funds/Money Market	Friend/Relative Re-Payment
Stocks/Bonds	Advance Payment
College Funds	Other
401(k)/403(b)/TSP	
Other (IRAs, etc.)	

REAL ESTATE	MORTGAGE BALANCE DUE
Home	Home
Rental Property	Rental Property
Other (Vac Home/Trailer/Time Share)	Other (Vac Home/Trailer/Time Share
TOTAL ASSETS $_____	TOTAL LIABILITIES $_____

NET WORTH $_____

MONTHLY INCOME

Salary Base Pay	$
Bonus Incentive/Special Pay	$
Allowance	$
Child Support	$
Banking Dividends	$
Allotments	$
Other Income (SSI/Rental Income/Welfare/etc.)	$

MONTHLY SPENDING

Savings & Investments	$
Automobile	$
Child Care	$
Clothing	$
Contributions	$
Education	$
Food	$
Gifts	$
Healthcare	$
Household	$
Insurance	$
Job Expenses	$
Leisure	$
Personal Care	$
Pet Care	$
Utilities	$
Miscellaneous	$
Creditors	$

MONTHLY BUDGET

SAVINGS	*ACTUAL*	*PROJECTED*
Emergency Fund (1-3 Months)		
Reserve		
Goal Getter Fund		
Investments/IRA/TSP/etc.		

LIVING EXPENSE	*ACTUAL*	*PROJECTED*
Auto		
Gas		
Maintenance Repair		
Other		
Child Care		
Allowance		
Day Care		
Support		
Clothing		
Laundry/Dry Cleaning		
Purchase ($50 month per person)		
Contributions		
Charities		
Club Dues/Association Fees		
Religious (Tithe/Offering)		

Education	
Books	
Fees (Other/Room & Board)	
Tuition	
Food	
Dining Out	
Groceries	
Lunch	
Vending Machines	
Meal Deduction	
Gifts	
Holidays	
Birthdays/Anniversaries	
Healthcare/Dental	
Eye Care	
Hospital/Physician	
Prescription	
Household	
Furnishing	
Maintenance Repair	
Mortgage/Rent	
Taxes/Fee	

Insurance
Automobile
Health/Dental
Homeowner/Rental
Life
Job Expenses
Non-Reimbursed
Reimbursed
Leisure
Athletic Events/Sporting Goods
Books & Magazines
Computer Product Software/Hardware
DVD/VHS & Video Games Rental
DVD's & CD's
Entertaining
Lessons
Toys & Games
Travel & Lodging
Personal Care
Barber/Beauty Shop
Beer/Liquor/Wine
Tobacco Products
Other _____
Pet Care
Food/Supplies
Veterinarian Service (Boarding/Grooming)

Utilities
Cable/Satellite TV
Cellular/Pager/Phone Cards
Electricity
Internet Service
Natural Gas/Propane
Telephone (Local & Long Distance)
Water/Garbage/Sewage
Miscellaneous
ATM Fees/Stamps/etc.
Other (Recommend $50-$150 Buffer)
TOTAL MONTHLY EXPENSE: _____   _____

Note: The monthly expense (including the amount in the savings category) shouldn't exceed 70% of your total income.

ACTION PLAN

List your proposed options in meeting your goal to Financial Freedom.

How will you increase your income:

1. _____

2. _____

3. _____

How will you decrease your living expenses:

1. _____

2. _____

3. _____

How will you decrease your indebtness:

1. _____

2. _____

3. _____

SPENDING PLAN

MONTHLY	1ST P / A	15th P / A
Savings & Investments		
Automobile		
Child Care		
Clothing		
Contributions		
Education		
Food		
Gifts		
Healthcare		
Household		
Insurance		
Job Expenses		
Leisure		
Personal Care		
Pet Care		
Utilities		
Miscellaneous		
Creditors		

POWER PAYMENT PLAN

Dr. Henry L. Armington, Sr. is available for special training with a minimum of 25 students.

Contact him for a group instructional aide presentation to financial freedom.

So . . . . on the mark, get set, ready GO!!!

Note: Each student must have in their possession a purchased copy of *"How To Get Your Hands Out The Lion Mouth."*

ORDER FORM

Use this convenient order form to purchase additional autographed books of
"HOW TO GET YOUR HANDS OUT THE LION MOUTH"

Please Print:
Name _____
Address _____
City _____ State _____
Zip _____
Phone ( )_____ Email _____

_____ copy of book(s) at $20.00 each = $_____
Shipping and Handling @ $5.00 per triple (3) book order = $_____
Total Enclosed $_____

Make personal/cashier checks and money orders payable to:
Henry Armington Ministries
P.O. Box 44545
Shreveport, LA 71134-4545

Note: Please allow 4-6 weeks for delivery of shipped material from Henry Armington Ministries.

OTHER BOOKS
BY
HENRY ARMINGTON

How To Save Your Marriage Without Losing Your Mind
This book is designed to be the foundation for marriages and homes to remain focused on the purpose behind why and how it commenced. It is the author's hope and ambition that through reading the contents therein, both single and married couple's will receive a better concept of how God planned for the relationship to be from the beginning to the end of time.

Never fail to capture the biblical text because only what you do for Christ will last. Relationships begin with the intent to last "Till death do us part," but oftentimes Satan shows up, leaving the couple in disbelief. In sections, you will experience how to confront the issue and get on with your life through the realization of how Satan functions in each of our lives.

You Can't Have My Song
This book is the humble effort to bring together under one cover and convenient size the essential concern for most conversations from God to mankind. One of the most tragic results in life is many people feel no one understands their inner struggles. The inner hurt, anger, and confusion about emotions cause many victims to feel their Father is either disgusted and hateful or completely uninvolved. As a result, they either work to make themselves acceptable through legalistic performance or turn their backs on God, assuming he has neglect hearing their song.

You should never underestimate the importance of singing praise. It's one of the most powerful spiritual weapons you have. Praise is more than a pleasant song or a few uplifting words about God. It releases the very presence of God, himself. You may have to sing through tear strained eyes, pain and suffering or a life filled with dark clouds, but keep on singing, praising and worshipping the Master. Even when you don't feel like singing, sing anyhow. And like Paul and Silas, you'll find the earth shaking, the prison doors of fear and doubt swinging open to liberate you in the Spirit of God.

***Available from your local bookstore
or online at Amazon.com***

"DREAMER'S GIVING" PLEDGE FORM

Goal: Request 700 people to pledge $1,000 or 350 people pledge $2,000 toward kingdom building this year. All donations are appreciated and tax deductible. Thank you for participating in the movement of Jesus Christ!

Name: _____

Address: _____

Phone #: _____

Email: _____

Adult Pledges
(19 years and up)

□$2,500   □$900

□$2,000   □$700

□$1,500   □$500

□$1,000   □$_____

Youth Pledges
(18 years and under)

□$300   □$100

□$200   □$_____

MEET THE AUTHOR

To contact Dr. Henry L. Armington, Sr. for preaching and/or speaking engagements, write:

Dr. Henry L. Armington, Sr.

P.O. Box 44545

Shreveport, Louisiana 71134-4545

Or

DrArmington.org

Or

DrArmington@cs.com

Please include your prayer request and comments when writing.

www.ingramcontent.com/pod-product-compliance
Lightning Source LLC
Chambersburg PA
CBHW020535290526
45786CB00002B/895